BRITAIN IN OLD PH

DARLINGTON
PAST & PRESENT

CHARLIE EMETT

SUTTON PUBLISHING

Sutton Publishing,
an imprint of NPI Media Group Limited
Cirencester Road · Chalford · Stroud
Gloucestershire · GL6 8PE

First published 2007

Title page photograph: Blackwellgate in 1934.

British Library Cataloguing in Publication Data
A catalogue record for this book is available from the British Library.

ISBN 978-07509-4620-9

Typeset in 10.5/13.5 Photina.
Typesetting and origination by
NPI Media Group Limited.
Printed and bound in England.

CONTENTS

Acknowledgements

Perusing the *Northern Echo* picture library is a most enjoyable occupation and my special thanks go to the managing director of the *Northern Echo*, Mr David Kelly and to Mr Peter Barron, editor of this great daily of the north for allowing me so to do. My thanks also go to Christine Watson, lovely guardian of these archives. All the pictures are courtesy of the *Northern Echo* except for two of the Joseph Pease statue, which are from Ron Dodsworth, whom I thank. A special thank you to Ken Dodd, OBE, for permission to use his view of the Civic Theatre. Thank you, all the helpful staff of Darlington Public Library, especially Christine Roe, a treasure if ever there was one. Thank you, Pam Gibson of Eagle Graphics for once again transforming my scrawl into type. It is always a pleasure working with Sutton Publishing's brilliant editorial team, formerly led by Senior Commissioning Editor Simon Fletcher. You are a strong and very professional team. If I have omitted anyone, I have done so inadvertently and I apologise. Should there be any errors, they are mine.

1 Early Days

Until the beginning of the nineteenth century, most of the people of Great Britain lived in the country and depended on agriculture for a living. In 1800 the population of County Durham was just short of 150,000 and Darlington, with a population of around 11,500, ranked eighth in size below the city of Durham.

Darlington is sited on the River Skerne at the first crossing point upstream of its confluence with the River Tees, 18 miles south of Durham City. It has occupied that site for some 2,000 years, most of that time as a village. During those long years its name has been spelled in different ways, all of which identified Darlington either as the homestead of Deornod's people or as a watery meadow. Legend has it that an early name for the River Skerne was Derning and this would have made it feasible for the village to have been given Dernington as a derivative name for Darlington.

Although Darlington had been established for some time, before William the Conqueror made his two-volume Domesday Book in 1068, the village was not included in it because it was situated north of the River Tees and outside William's control.

From its earliest days, the Prince Bishops of Durham had been lords of the manor of Darlington, which gave them vice-regal powers, including the right to levy taxes and to grant market charters.

In the tenth century, the coffin of St Cuthbert was rested in Darlington by monks taking it to Chester-le-Street. To commemorate this event, the present church of St Cuthbert was built towards the end of the twelfth century. It was built on or near an earlier Saxon church.

The earlier Saxon church was still in existence in the early eleventh century. Between 1003 and 1016, Styr, an influential Danish noble in Northumbria, gave lands including 'Dearnington' to the Episcopal See of Durham 'for St. Cuthbert.' It is unlikely that this church survived the Danish invasions, the invasion of the North by William the Conqueror and raids by Malcolm of Scotland in 1072.

There was probably no church there by 1080, but it is almost certain that there was a Norman church there during the episcopate of William of St Calais who, in 1083, displaced the secular or married priests from the Benedictine Priory of Durham and found homes for some of them in Darlington.

At the same time he elevated St Cuthbert's to a collegiate church. So now it supported a vicar and four prebends. The latter's stipends came from the lands and property in various parts of the parish.

The small Norman church was superseded by a larger one which Bishop Puiset and his architects built from its foundations. Building began in 1180 and work was still in progress in 1192, according to Geoffrey of Goldingham's *History of Churches in Durham from 1152 to 1214.*

Darlington's market place, bounded by Headrow, Tubwell Row, Horsemarket and St Cuthbert's churchyard was probably laid out in about 1164 when Bishop Pudsey built a manor house beside the Skerne.

In the twelfth century, Darlington was raised to the status of one of the bishop's boroughs and this gave it the right to hold markets. For several centuries the township of Darlington covered an area of 3,000 acres, extending approximately 3 miles east to west and 2 miles north to south. Its built-up area covered about 140 acres and the town's prosperity depended on its status as a market town. It thrived on the production of leather and the manufacture of woollen and linen cloth.

The town's two prominent Quaker families, Backhouse and Pease, had been founded on flax and wool respectively. The Backhouse family soon diversified into banking but the Pease family interest remained in the ever-expanding textile industry. By the fourteenth century, wealthy Darlington wool merchants were exporting wool to Flanders, via the port of Newcastle and were much involved in weaving, fulling and dyeing woollen cloth. So successful were the Darlington wool merchants, that by 1380 Darlington was by far the wealthiest among the neighbouring boroughs of Gateshead, Sunderland and Durham.

In 1585 some 273 houses were destroyed in Darlington when a fierce fire swept through the town, gutting High Row and Skinnergate and making eighty people homeless. Only buildings in the lower part of the town escaped.

The great fire happened at a time when the wool trade in Darlington was beginning to decline. Leather was the up and coming industry with weavers outnumbered by leather workers in the town.

Royalty first visited Darlington in 1617 in the shape of James I, who stayed at the Crown Inn. While there, he saw the town for what it was and expressed his view of it.

'Darnton! I think it is Darnton i't dirt.'

Thanks, in part, to his honest opinion, Darlington was later cleaned, but not right away. It was still a filthy town in the mid-eighteenth century, by which time its population had grown to over 3,000, thanks to the continuing growth of the wool and textile industries. By 1800, more than 5,000 people were living in Darlington.

The early years of the nineteenth century saw the greatest change in the history of Darlington. It all began with the opening of the Stockton & Darlington Railway, the first railway to be worked by steam, on 27 September 1825. That, for Darlington, marked the beginning of the Industrial Revolution. That was how the advent of the railways transformed Darlington from a market town into an industrial centre. That was how Darlington became a railway town.

The Bailiffs of Darlington 1299 to 1867.

Bailiffs of Darlington

1299–1867.

1299 — Eldam de Sulton	Robert Dearham
1315 — Robert de Darlington	1615 — Michael Atkinson
1361 — Nicholas de Belgrave	1617 — Geo Richardson
1386 — John de Midleton	1619 — John Lisle
1418 — Robert Belasys	1625 — Thomas Barnes
1420 — William Elwent	1626 — Richard Matthews
1437 — John Spence	1651 — John Middleton
1447 — John Sharpe	1658 — Christopher Place
1457 — Thomas Rycheburn	Thomas Blakiston
1457 — William Eland	1669 — William Burletson
1461 — William Clayton	1680 — Michael Blackett
1467 — Roland Thirkeld	1698 — Richard Hilton
Thomas Haidok	Matthew Lamb
1476 — Henry Sale	1710 — Daniel Moore
1494 — John Perkynson	Charles Moore
1501 — William Bettys	1736 — Benjamin Hilton
1514 — Richard Waldgrave	Geo Keenliside
1516 — Thomas T	1753 — Ralph Robson
1528 — William Wytham	1774 — Henry Ornsby
1535 — Tunstall	1806 — Geo Ornsby
1558 — Thomas Vaux	1816 — Thomas Bowes
1558 — Laurence Thornell	1828 — Christopher Sherwood
1561 — Ralph Eure	1846 to 1867 — Francis Mewburn
William Barnes	
1591 — Christopher Barnes	
1606 — Robert Ward	

A witch on ducking stool on the River Skerne, alongside where Northgate was to develop.

A sixteenth-century well discovered on the site of Darlington's £5 million recreation centre. Houses of consequence at about this time all had wells.

The site director at the Darlington archaeological dig, November 1994.

Darlington's market cross, erected by Dame
Dorothy Broam in 1727.

The bridge over the River Skerne at
Darlington, 1760.

The bishop's palace, Darlington, 1764.

The bridge over the River Skerne at Darlington, 1767, backed by St Cuthbert's church.

The tollbooth on the site of the town clock. The tollbooth was demolished in 1808.

Front elevation of houses in Northgate, Darlington in 1848.

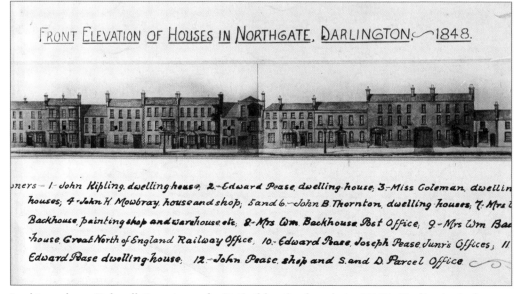

FRONT ELEVATION OF HOUSES IN NORTHGATE. DARLINGTON. 1848.

oners – 1- John Kipling. dwelling house. 2.– Edward Pease, dwelling-house; 3-Miss Coleman, dwellin
houses; 4-John H. Mowbray, house and shop; 5 and 6.– John B. Thornton, dwelling-houses; 7.-Mrs
Backhouse, painting shop and warehouse etc. 8-Mrs Wm. Backhouse Post Office. 9.– Mrs Wm Bac
-house, Great North of England Railway Office, 10.- Edward Pease, Joseph Pease Junr's Offices; 11
Edward Pease dwelling-house; 12-John Pease, shop and S. and D. Parcel Office

Looking along Tubwell Row towards St Cuthbert's church in 1848. Darlington's famous clock tower and covered market had yet to be built at this time.

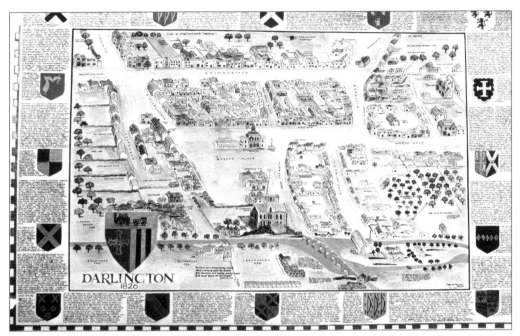

The layout of Darlington centre, 1826.

Mrs Ena Smith of Holmlands Road, Darlington, with her picture of Darlington centre as it looked in the early nineteenth century.

The covered market, dominated by Darlington's clock tower, a gift from Joseph Pease. The old town hall, to the right of the picture, the covered market and the clock tower were all designed by the famous architect, Alfred Waterhouse. The whole building was completed in 1864.

Blackwell in the 1880s.

A Christmas card dated 1888, showing Darlington scenes.

A picture of old Darlington, *c.* 1890.

Faverdale, now occupied by a supermarket.

Darlington's first tram car, being driven by the mayoress in 1904.

Darlington's historic borough book.

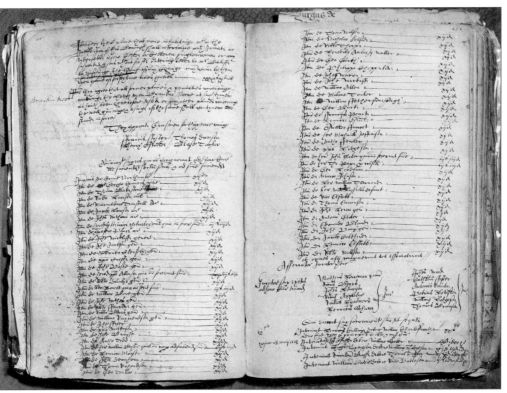

2   *Full Steam Ahead*

During the eighteenth century, coal from the seaward dipping mines of the Tyne hinterland was easily extracted and transported along short waggonways to the navigable Tyne and Wear rivers. Coal from the South Durham coalfield around Bishop Auckland on the other hand, was even easier to mine but although available in millions of tons per annum, was limited to thousands of tons because the coal was usually conveyed on pack horses, mules and asses, an expensive and inefficient means of transport.

There were two practical alternatives to road transport for the conveyance of minerals, goods and passengers – canals and railways.

By the late 1780s many of Britain's early canals had been built and the country was caught up in canal mania. Then in 1793, Britain went to war with France and this caused inflation, resulting in canal construction costing more and taking longer to complete. The future was fraught with difficulties and uncertainty.

On 13 September 1801 at a dinner held in Stockton's Town Hall, Leonard Raisbeck, Stockton's recorder, moved a resolution that a committee be appointed to enquire into the feasibility of building a railway or canal from Stockton to Winston via Darlington for the carriage of mineral and other traffic from North Yorkshire and South Durham.

In 1811 the appointed committee agreed that either a canal or a railway would be of great advantage to the locality.

On Friday 17 January 1812 at a meeting held at the King's Head, Darlington, it was resolved to employ the eminent engineer, Rennie, to survey the route and to explore the options, which he did in 1813.

For six years public opinion was divided as to whether a canal or railway would best serve the interests of commerce and benefit the proprietors; and the canal had the advantage. For various reasons, no progress was made one way or the other.

On 13 July at a public meeting held in Stockton, Leonard Raisbeck, the principal speaker, recommended that the canal should commence at the north end of Stockton and go via Darlington to Winston Bridge. The nature of the land the canal would have to cross was unfavourable with fifty locks required in under 30 miles and the estimated cost came to £205,233; double that of the suggested cost of the proposed railway.

On 4 September 1818 at a meeting in Darlington, a committee was appointed to consider the relative merits of those advocating a canal and those promoting a railway.

On 13 September 1818, at a meeting in Darlington Town Hall, reports of Mr Rennie on the canal scheme and of Mr Overton for the railway, were read separately. A report was also presented on the relative merits of the two schemes. The principal speakers were Jonathan Backhouse, Edward Pease, John Grimshaw and William Stobart Junior, each of whom strongly recommended the adoption of a railway in preference to a canal.

In 1818 railway engineer George Overton was employed to survey the original line because there was still a good deal of uncertainty about the route the railway should take. The first route chosen on Overton's recommendation and survey was from Stockton via Darlington, Summerhouse, Ingleton and Hilton to the West Auckland coalfields, cutting through one of the Duke of Cleveland's fox coverts, which was of greater concern to the nobility than the promoters of a public railway.

Overton undertook another survey, which was completed by 1 September 1820. On 29 September 1820 he submitted a report to the committee, who endorsed his observation in a manifesto dated November 1820. The manifesto showed that the expense of construction a railway track on the intended line was estimated at £82,000, the greater part of which was subscribed.

An application for an act authorising the construction of the Stockton & Darlington Railway was delayed owing to the death of King George III. The S&DR Company fought as hard for the second bill as for the first, attempting to influence as many supporters as possible. Their efforts met with success and the second bill received royal assent in April 1821.

The man who more that anyone promoted the passing of the act authorising the construction of the S&DR was Edward Pease, 'the father of the railways.'

The S&DR's first act contained no powers for the use of locomotives, whereas in the company's second act they were empowered to 'make, erect and set up one permanent fixed steam engine or other proper machine in such convenient situation' as they chose.

On 23 May 1822 Thomas Meynell of Yarm, chairman of the S&DR, cut what he thought was the first sod of the new railway line. But this was not so, for one evening in the autumn of 1821, while busily engaged on the line's survey, and finding himself surrounded by some of the workmen, George Stephenson said, 'Come, give me a spade. Let it never be said that I have not made a beginning.' There and then, close to St John's well, he began work on the new railway.

During the late summer of 1825 *Locomotion No. 1* arrived at Aycliffe level, carried on a trolley. It was placed on the rails, its boiler filled with water and the wood and coal was made ready for lighting when it was discovered that no one had a light. At that time matches were virtually unheard of. George Stephenson, designer and builder of his own locomotives, was about to send a man to Aycliffe for a lighted lantern when Robert Metcalfe, a navvy, stepped forward and gave him a burning glass, saying that as he always lit his pipe with it, perhaps it might fire the engine. Stephenson invited him to try, and using the burning glass and a piece of tarred oakum, Metcalfe lit the fire of *Locomotion No. 1*.

A coach, ordered by the Stockton & Darlington Company, was built at Newcastle and delivered on 20 September 1825. It was the first passenger coach ever built. It was called *Experiment* and was intended to travel daily between Darlington and Stockton. It was coupled to *Locomotion No. 1* and on the morning of 25 September 1825, several members of the committee had a ride in it from Shildon to Darlington, thereby travelling in the first ever railway carriage. They were Edward Pease Senior, Edward Pease Junior, Joseph Pease, Henry Pease, Thomas Richardson, William Kitching and George Stephenson, whose brother James drove the engine.

On Tuesday 27 September 1825, *Locomotion No. 1*, preceded by a flag-waving man on a horse, began its precursory journey from the foot of Brusselton incline to Stockton, pulling its tender – six wagons of coal and merchandise, the company coach, carrying the committee and other proprietors, six wagons with seats reserved for passengers and fourteen wagons for the conveyance of workers.

The train arrived at Stockton at 3.45 pm to a salute of seven guns and Meynell's band immediately struck up 'God save the King'. Congratulations continued unabated for many hours yet by a sad twist of fate, Edward Pease, who more than anyone else had brought the S&DR into being, was absent from the celebrations. His son, in his twenties, had died. The whole Pease family was in mourning and kept away.

Although the world's first steam-operated public railway carried passengers for the first time on the 27 September 1825, and although *Locomotion No. 1* reached the unprecedented speed of 15 mph, the passengers who continued to be transported along the track did so in horse-drawn coaches until 1837.

Separate services for freight and passengers were not introduced until 1836.

North Road station did not come into being at the same time as the opening of the S&DR. Before the railways had developed properly, there was no need for stations. Passengers used horse-drawn services that stopped at inns; and this practice continued for several years after *Locomotion No. 1*'s inaugural journey. Moreover, the S&DR did not hold passengers in high regard. Transport of coal was the number one priority.

The station which sufficed for Darlington from 1837 until 1842 was a small goods warehouse comprising a booking office, waiting room and cottage, with a narrow wooden platform, approached by a flight of steps from the east side of North Road, near Skerne Bridge.

In 1842 it was replaced by a new North Road station, which was sited west of North Road itself. It is believed to be the oldest railway station in the world. By 1850 the original station cottage had been demolished and a coal cellar had been built on the site. One winter's night in 1850, James Durham, a night watchman, was on duty at North Road station. Having completed one inspection and feeling cold and hungry, he went down some steps to the porter's cellar, where there was a fire and a gas light. The coal cellar was adjacent to the porter's room.

Durham sat on a bench facing the fire and was about to eat when a strange man, followed by a large black retriever entered from the coal cellar. The man wore a smart cutaway coat with gilt buttons and a stand-up collar. The two men stared at each other. Then, his eyes still on Durham, the stranger moved in front of the fireplace. He watched Durham with a curious smile on his face, then struck him. Durham struck him back and 'my hand passed through him and skinned the knuckles on the fireplace.' The man fell back towards the fire and the dog attacked Durham, hurting his leg, but leaving no bite marks. The stranger recovered, clicked his tongue at the dog and returned to the coal cellar. Durham lit his lantern and followed. There was no way out, but there was no sign of either man or dog. The story was checked. What Durham did not know was that a railway man called Winter, owner of a black dog, shot himself in the vicinity. He had been dressed as Durham had seen him and his body had lain undetected in the cellar for some time. The ghost has not appeared since, but today there is a trap door in the main platform that gives access to the cellar.

North Road station was built as a single-storey building, but in 1873 it was given a first floor and enlarged to incorporate an adjoining carriage shed.

At first, North Road station had three tracks running into it, but only one carried trains in both directions. During the mid-nineteenth century further modifications were made and in 1894 two bays were removed to allow two tracks to run through the station on either side of a platform, reached by a wooden bridge.

During the decades following the Second World War services using North Road station were gradually reduced, leaving the area west of Darlington increasingly cut off from the railway network. By 1972, only one line ran through North Road station, going as far as Bishop Auckland, just a few miles out of town. Now an unmanned halt, North Road station was in serious danger of being closed down. Turning North Road station into an unmanned halt and the reduction in trains using it caused serious problems. Deprived of rail staff, it deteriorated from being a several-times winner of Best Kept Station awards to becoming a target for vandals. Windows were smashed, fixtures and fittings were ripped out and at one point it was subjected to an arson attack. Rough winter weather played its part and before long the station became little more than a derelict shell.

In the 1930s, a German Jew, Herbert Wolfe, and his brother fled the Nazis. They came to England and established a successful chemical manufacturing factory at Newton Aycliffe. Herbert gained a reputation as a champion of what appeared to be lost causes, one of which was North Road station. He felt that it should not be allowed to remain ruinous and, in 1969, invited a number of local people, including businessmen and local government representatives to support his efforts to save the building.

They came up with the idea of a railway museum and began consultations with the local authority, the forerunner of Darlington Borough Council, with a view to having the project managed as a joint partnership with local preservationists.

Northumbria Tourist Board, recognising the potential of a museum as a tourist attraction, also gave its support. Protracted negotiations followed which lasted until

July 1973, when it was decided to first of all restore North Road station, before converting it into a museum.

Restoring the dilapidated station was a daunting task but thanks to a lot of hard work by contractors, council staff and volunteers alike, the museum was ready for the opening by Prince Philip, Duke of Edinburgh, on 27 September 1975, exactly 150 years after *Locomotion No. 1* had made its historic first journey.

Although the borough council supported the museum it was run, in 1975, by the Darlington Railway Museum Trust, a registered charity set up in 1974. Following the royal opening, work continued apace, partly because of dedicated volunteers and government schemes which enabled the use of unemployed craftsmen.

By 1985 the council had increased its grant aid, which averted the threat of closure and made available help from Alan Suddes, curator of the town's museum. Furthermore, it was now possible to appoint a full time administrator – Steven Dyke.

The museum contains a very large collection of railway memorabilia, bequeathed by Ken Hoole, honorary curator in the museum's early days.

Today with diesel and electricity having usurped steam, North Road Museum reminds us of the days when steam was king!

In 1835 Joseph Pease, son of Edward Pease, began to make plans for a railway line that would link Darlington with York. He had visions of opening up a route to London, using existing and proposed lines. These, he envisaged, would also increase the possibility of selling coal throughout the North Riding of Yorkshire.

In 1841, as a result of Joseph Pease's bold scheme, Darlington was connected to York by the Great North of England Railway. There were seven trains a day from Darlington's tiny station to York and because there were few curves on the line, these trains were the fastest in England.

Because Darlington's new station was situated at Bank Top, it was called Bank Top station. When in 1887, a new, much larger station was opened on the same site, the original Bank Top station was built into the new one and, in effect, vanished. This new, larger station was given a new name, Central station, but eventually the station reverted to its original name Bank Top.

The new Bank Top station remains today as large as the original Bank Top station was small. Platform four, its main Down platform is 500yds long and is set behind stout iron railings. It is reached through strongly guarded gates above which are suspended notices giving the destination and character of the next train due to depart the platform to which the gates give access. Platform four is the one at which the main line trains from London King's Cross to the north are invariably accommodated.

Along the centre of the station, parallel to the Up and Down lines, is a row of buildings containing the waiting and refreshment room, luggage and parcels offices, booking office, the District Superintendent's office, toilets, etc. They are all signposted.

Between the north end of the row of station buildings and the barrier of the Down platform there is an area about 16 yds long adjoining these platforms. People frequently congregate in this area where all types of reading material can be purchased from a W.H. Smith stall. Refreshments can also be purchased from an adjacent stall, while overhead electrically-operated timetables keep everyone informed of train arrival and departure times.

The two main platforms are not reserved for the main line expresses alone. They also accommodate certain trains for West Durham, Tebay, Penrith, Leeds, Harrogate, Richmond, Saltburn, Middlesbrough, Scarborough and so on.

Generally speaking, platform one is used to accommodate trains going south and east and platform four is for those going north or west.

Between platform four and the west wall of the station are two sets of rails. The set nearest the platform is the main Down line and the outside set is an independent line. The two lines are connected to each other in such a way that a fast train may, by use of the independent line, pass a slow train standing alongside the south part of platform four, cross to the main line and be accommodated at the other end of the same long platform, resuming its journey in front of the 'slow'. This method of working is used every day.

Between platform one and the eastern wall of the station are three sets of rails, the main line and an independent similar to the one mentioned above and a siding on which is kept a spare bogie set. This is a train of bogie carriages ready for service in case pressure of traffic or other causes make it necessary to duplicate any of the through expresses. Two express engines, one facing north, the other south, are also kept in readiness at the station to give assistance when required.

Platforms three and four are comparatively short and run parallel with the main platforms and with each other, either being the inner parts of platforms one and four respectively.

They serve dock or loading lines laid centrally between the south ends of the main platforms. Platforms five and six are at the north end of platform four and reached from it.

How different all this is from Darlington's original Bank Top station, which did not amuse Queen Victoria when she visited Darlington on 28 May 1849. She pointed out that for the main line station of the very place in which the railway had been born to look so down-at-heel was just not good enough. The Great North of England Railway, whose station it was, was shamed into making some improvements. But another 38 years were to pass before Darlington's present railway station was built at a cost of £110,000 in 1887.

Darlington's two railway stations did not develop accident-free. In 1910 there was a collision at Bank Top station in which an engine was toppled. There was no loss of life at this one. Sadly, despite stringent safety measures, a collision occurred at North Road station which resulted in the deaths of two people. This happened on 9 March 1929.

By and large both North Road and Bank Top stations have weathered the steam age very well. North Road station was much involved with *Locomotion No. 1* when it made its inaugural journey on 27 September 1825 and Bank Top had a long association with *Mallard*, the greatest steam locomotive in the world, which travelled at a speed of 125mph between Grantham and Peterborough, achieving a world record for steam traction that has never been beaten. Both Darlington's railway stations have excellent associations with the world of steam.

Although North Road station was sited at the Darlington end of the S&DR, all repairs to the locomotives were done at Shildon. This method worked for a while, but became increasingly difficult as Shildon shops became inundated with work. In 1854, John Dixon, the S&DR engineer, suggested to the S&DR director that the time had come to consider future locations for the locomotive works and headquarters. For three years this was discussed before a decision was reached that the new works should be at Darlington. Land costing £9,139 9s 4d was bought and William Bouch, a locomotive engineer, was put in charge of planning the new workshops.

North Road Locomotive Works, Darlington, was opened on 1 January 1863, by the S&DR, which, at that time, owned 128 locomotives. It was expected that the S&DR would increase the figure to 260 by 1891.

In 1891 the North Eastern Railway Company owned 1,560 pieces of stock, locomotives, wagons, etc., many of which were maintained at Darlington.

North Road Locomotive Works was known locally as North Road shops. It was located on North Road, part of the Edinburgh–London stagecoach route, within easy reach of North Road and Bank Top stations. It covered an area of about 6 acres with a further 27 acres of land purchased for extension.

In 1867 a new store house was built and in 1876 a new boiler shop was added. In 1884 a new forge and two new erecting shops were put up. In 1898 new stores offices, mess rooms and extensions to the brass foundry were built. In 1903 a second erecting shop was built and in 1911 a new paint shop and boiler and tender shop were erected at Stooperdale to relieve congestion at the North Road Shops.

The building of passenger engines at the erecting shop, North Road shops, began in 1871 and the first one was No. 1238, 4–4–0 intended for use on the Darlington to Tebay line over Stainmore.

During the First World War the erecting shop was renamed No. 1 machine shop, and the work done there was concentrated on items needed for the war with Germany. In August 1915 the Darlington Projectile Factory was opened. It was built at government expense but managed by the NER on the understanding that at the end of the war it would be taken over by the North Eastern. This became No. 2 machine shop. In time, North Road shops maintained and overhauled 499 passenger and 1,481 freight engines.

In February 1928 Darlington began building the frames for the famous No. 10,000 *Hush Hush* engine. The frames were built at North Road shops and the water tube boilers came from the specialist firm of Yarrow of Glasgow. The frames were sent to Glasgow to have the boilers mounted and, when ready to be returned to Darlington, the engines were covered in sheets to protect them from prying LMS eyes.

North Road shops, along with the rest of the railways, was nationalised on 1 January 1948, and the changes this brought about soon became apparent. By 1950 engines were being built to LMS designs. Then engines to BR standard design started coming out of North Road shops. They were followed by the first Darlington-built diesel electric. In December 1952, the first engines to BR standard designs were built. These were No. 78,000 2–6–0s. The BR diesel electric shunter appeared in August 1953. Together these provided a livelihood for North Road Shops until August 1964. In the 106 years of its existence North Road shops built 2,775 new locomotives.

The number of men employed at North Road shops in 1864 was 150. Over the years this grew to almost 4,000, but over the last few years of its existence the numbers dropped until only a skeleton staff was left.

North Eastern Railway
emblem.

A passenger train at
platform one, Darlington
Bank Top, February 1931.

Platform four, Darlington Bank Top, which is usually used to accommodate trains going north or west.

Bill Lake, BR's area manager at Darlington until he retired, polishing Bank Top station's huge bronze bell, watched by Councillor Jim Skinner, Councillor Mrs Joan Farey and BR's area manager, Chris Dickinson. The bell was originally sited on Bank Top station's Victorian clocktower.

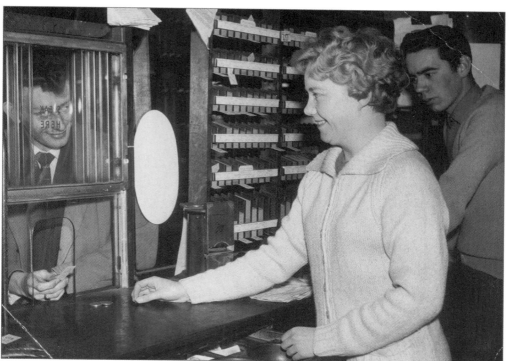

'For you, love, only £4.' That's the ticket. The passenger on the right can't believe it. Darlington Bank Top booking office, 1961.

This is not how platform staff view passengers boarding and alighting from trains at Bank Top station. This scene is of cattle at Bank Top cattle bay.

The south end of Darlington Bank Top, showing the locomotion depot in 1938, at the time of its reconstruction.

Off your bike – let the train take the strain. Darlington Bank Top, platform four, looking south.

Signalmen Tony Lands and Gerald Auty in the signal-box at Bank Top station.

An Intercity 125 heading south from Bank Top station, 1987.

Darlington North Road station, 1968. In 1858 the first railway drinking fountain was installed at North Road station in the interests of sobriety, to provide pure drinking water for the benefit of the wayfaring public.

A plaque showing the six visionaries who initiated the Stockton & Darlington Railway. The railway was originated in 1825 and started a transport revolution.

A shot of Stephenson's *Locomotion No. 1*.

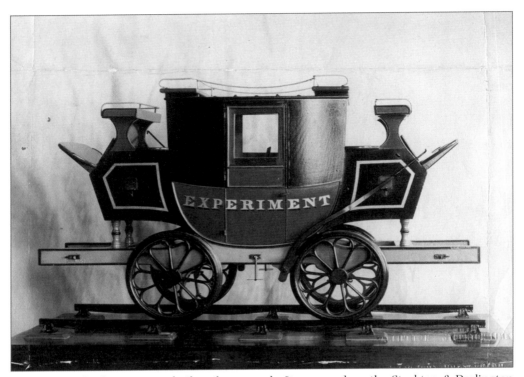

Experiment, the first purpose-built railway coach. It was used on the Stockton & Darlington Railway.

The first railway carriage with more than one compartment: this one had three, the top of each compartment being just above the heads of the passengers. This S&DR carriage was in use between 1840 and 1850.

North Road station, Darlington, on a quiet day in 1972.

Mrs Edith Bowe on duty behind the counter of the souvenir shop at North Road station.

Mock horror etched on their faces, two ghost-hunters prepare for an encounter with the phantom of a railwayman who killed himself at North Road station.

Railway Queen Brenda Tomlinson and Darlington's mayor, Joe Peterson, bring a touch of civic pride to highly polished engine No. 1275 at North Road station, 1975.

This railwaymen's reunion of the 8 September 1994, at North Road station was, as the sign has it, 'way out'.

North Road Locomotive Works open day, 29 July 1954.

Darlington scrap depot, part of North Road Locomotive Works, where all the local steam engines were broken up, June 1960.

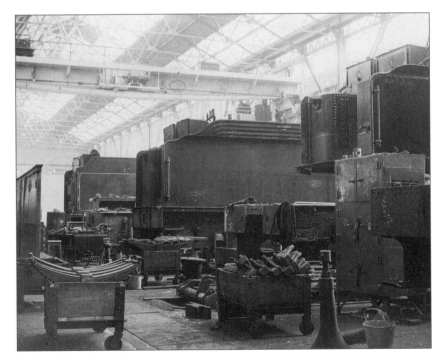

Scene of an explosion at North Road Locomotive Works, 15 February 1961.

By 1962 the severe closures brought about by Dr Beeching were beginning to bite. They affected most aspects of railway life, including North Road shops. Those employed there held a protest march on 6 September 1962 pictured here, it shows the measure of the protest.

Despite redundancy problems, Darlington Locomotive Works management staff held their annual dinner dance on Friday 7 February 1964. Hope springs eternal.

Lord Hailsham talking to a deputation from North Road Locomotive Works when he visited Darlington Town Hall on 9 February 1963.

The frontage of North Road shops, as far right as the clock, October 1973.

The frontage of what was North Road Shops, now Morrisons supermarket, 3 April 1991. The smell of change hangs heavy in the air.

Len Palmer leaving North Road Shops (Locomotive Works) for the last time, 22 August 1964.

A sad end to North Road shops, with only the faithful cat remaining, 2 April, 1966.

3   Floreat Industria

O ne family more than any other influenced Darlington's transformation form
    market town to industrial centre. It was the Pease family and no industrial
    history of Darlington would be complete without mention of this illustrious
family. The involvement of the Peases began when, in the mid-eighteenth century,
the first Edward Pease, born in 1711, came to Darlington to work for his uncle,
Thomas Cauldwell, a wool comber, taking over and expanding the business to
include dyeing and weaving when his uncle died.

Edward Pease had, two mills on the River Skerne, one in the Leadyard and one in
Priestgate. In the early part of the nineteenth century, at least 10 per cent of
Darlington's population was employed in the woollen mills, which had now become
H. Pease and Company. In those early days the mill was more a centre of exchange
than for manufacture. Wool bought in country districts was brought to the mill for
sorting, washing and cleaning. It was then handed out to wool combers who combed
it in their own cottages. When this work was done, the combers returned the wool to
the mill and were paid a commission. A similar procedure was adopted for spinning.

Towards the end of the eighteenth century, the two brothers, Edward and Joseph
Pease, took over to the business. In 1817, the Leadyard Mill was destroyed by fire,
but the firm, now called Joseph Pease and Sons, gradually recovered from the fire
and quickly gained a reputation for fine craftsmanship. Later, in 1894, the
Priestgate Mill was badly damaged, also by fire.

From 1752 to 1902 the business was owned by a series of partnerships, all
involving the Pease family. In 1903, the firm became a private limited company
with some of the Pease family on the board of directors.

For many years there was a happy business relationship between Henry Pease
and Co. Ltd and Lister and Co. of Bradford; and, in 1920, Lister purchased all the
share capital of Henry Pease and appointed a new board of directors.

To all outward appearances, the mills seemed the same as they had been fifty
years before, but inside, steam power was supplanted by electricity.

On Sunday 2 July 1933, the wool warehouse at Pease's Mill burst into flames
and only the shell of the building remained. But thanks to the availability of
modern transport and the goodwill of their friends in Bradford, raw material was
available the next day and there was no loss of employment.

In 1790 Quaker William Kitching, a weaver, opened an ironmonger's shop in
Darlington's Tubwell Row. From that small beginning sprang Whessoe, an

international group of companies, which, at its height, employed over 20,000 people in its manufacturing plants, offices and on construction sites. Its reputation was built on the design, fabrication and construction of storage and treatment plant for the oil, gas and chemical industries, wind tunnels, nuclear vessels, hydro-electric power and navigation systems. It also manufactured plastic pressure vessels, beach huts and catamarans. Today, Whessoe concentrates on instrumentation and control, and project engineering.

In 1821, when the campaign to establish the Stockton & Darlington Railway was at its height, the Kitching family was very much involved in this development. William Kitching the younger, subscribed £400 to it. In 1823 he was elected to both the General Committee and a sub-committee, which had day-to-day control of the building of the S&DR.

By 1830 it was decided that Kitching's Tubwell Row shop was too small and the business was transferred to a new site further north. The railway foundry was established and called Whessoe Foundry. The new S&DR, with which the Kitchings had been involved, now became Whessoe Foundry's most important customer.

The name Whessoe is of Saxon origin and a Saxon village of that name existed more than 800 years ago about half a mile north of where Whessoe Foundry stood.

Until about 1890, Whessoe Foundry concentrated on the structural side of railway work and in 1891 saw the development of modern Whessoe. That same year the business was converted by the proprietors into a private company and in the following decade Whessoe began to build gas holders and tanks for the oil industry.

In 1921, Whessoe became a public company and began in earnest to provide the technical basis for its services and to expand those services to meet the needs of the particular industries with which it was concerned.

During the 1930s Whessoe became one of the leading manufacturers of gas plant. In 1934, it installed a pickling shop to remove mill-scale from tank plates, which made them more secure against corrosion. This development was copied throughout the UK, USA, France and elsewhere.

Also during the 1930s, Whessoe was at the forefront of the gradual changeover from riveting to welding. This proved to be a most important move in the company's progress.

By the beginning of the Second World War, Whessoe had become established as one of the leading companies in the country.

During the Second World War Whessoe had its own Home Guard Battalion under the command of Major Claude Spielmand, Managing Director of Whessoe, and every able-bodied male over the age of 18 was required to join.

During the 1940s, Whessoe's production was fully concentrated on the war effort.

When peace was declared a new peace time production line switched to heat exchanges which were designed by the Lummus Company, an American design organisation, with offices in London.

In about 1950, Whessoe was licensed to manufacture venting and measuring equipment for petroleum product storage tanks, from an American company, Shand and Jurs, in California. This product line was the forerunner of the light engineering side of Whessoe, now recognised as Whessoe Systems and Controls Ltd., which became the linchpin of the Whessoe Group.

The largest vessel ever to come out of the Whessoe works in one piece was a massive nitric acid vessel. It weighed 180 tons and was 38 metres long by 4.5 metres in diameter. It was being transported to Hartlepool Docks, Teesside.

In January 1994 the Whessoe Group Companies numbered twelve: five in England, three in the USA, one in Australia, one in France, one in Italy and one in Norway.

Darlington and Simpson Rolling Mills was originally called Fry I'Anson and Co. It built its Rise Carr works in 1862/3, the works opened in 1864 and the roof blew off in 1865! The original works consisted of a puddling forge, which converted pig iron to wrought iron by heating it with ferric oxide in a furnace to oxidise the carbon. It had one 16ft mill and one 10ft mill. Iron was the only product. In about 1870 an 8ft mill and another puddling forge were added. By the turn of the twentieth century, steel had begun to supersede iron and the works began to roll steel sections instead.

Darlington and Simpson Rolling Mills occupied three sites, which were designated South, North and West Works. In 1902 a rivet manufacturing shop was erected at the south end of the South Works. In 1930 it was removed to the North Works to make room for numbered one and two yards. In 1904 a mill was laid down for the rolling of light rails from old rails and billet crops. A forge was dismantled to make room for this mill.

That same year, 1904, Fry I'Anson and Co's name changed to Sir Theodore Fry and Co. and in 1910 the name changed again to Darlington Rolling Mills Co. Ltd. In 1911 there was a complete regrouping of Rise Carr Works. Everything was electrified except the 8ft mill, which continued to run under steam until it was dismantled in about 1924.

In 1917 a new rail mill was built to the north of the existing works. During the dark days of the 1930s, work at Darlington Rolling Mills slumped because of competition from cheaper, continental imports. A full week's work was now no longer a certainty.

In 1935 the company once more changed its name, this time to Darlington and Simpson Rolling Mills Ltd. The company continued to operate under this name for a further sixty-three years until 1998 when it closed down.

In 1877, Henry Isaac Dixon bought an interest in a 2-acre site at Smithfield Road, Darlington, and in 1882 Charles Frederick Dixon bought it outright. On 27 July 1898, he formed the Cleveland Bridge and Iron Co. Ltd.

The Smithfield Road site, opened in 1877, was Cleveland Bridge's base for the first sixty-odd years of its life. Almost all the work Cleveland Bridge did at its Smithfield Road base was designed for riveting, not welding. From its beginning in

1877, Cleveland Bridge expanded rapidly. In 1893 the company built its first overseas bridge in New South Wales, Australia. This was followed by a bridge over the River Negro/Amazon at Manaus in Brazil. Cleveland Bridge won its first major contract, worth £600,000, in 1902. This was for building the King Edward VII Bridge over the River Tyne. In 1904 its first significant overseas contract worth £72,000 was for the Victoria Falls Bridge across the Zambesi. This was followed in 1907 by a contract to build the Blue Nile Bridge at Khartoum. The Harding Bridge, which Cleveland Bridge built over the River Ganges in Bangladesh in 1912, is over 5,964ft long.

In the years before the Second World War, Cleveland Bridge built many bridges in places as far dispersed as South America, Africa, India, New Zealand and China. The company also supplied 15,000 tons of bridge for the French railways.

In 1967, C.C. Dixon, who had succeeded his father J.P. Dixon, decided that the future of the company would be best assured by becoming a subsidiary of a larger company. He arranged for shares to be purchased by the Cementation Construction Group, later acquired by Trafalgar House, which expanded its activities into the new offshore market, becoming Trafalgar Offshore Ltd.

In 1982 Cleveland Bridge moved from Smithfield Road to its present Yarm Road site. Today Cleveland Bridge is renowned as a world leader in bridge-building.

The American company Cummins came into being on 1 February 1918 and grew from a fledgling concern manufacturing what was then a new kind of engine for one of America's leading industrial corporations, whose engines provided power for over 700 applications in nearly every country in the world.

In 1964, a Chrysler Cummins factory was constructed at Darlington, and in mid-1965, the Cummins Engine factory was built alongside the Chrysler Cummins factory. The site of these two factories was at the eastern end of Darlington, alongside Yarm Road and covered an area of 640,000sq. ft. The two factories together were expected to provide almost 2,000 jobs for Darlington. Cummins Engines on its 240,000 sq. ft site, was intended to employ 700 men, working on a patent pressure-time fuel system and diesel components. The Chrysler Cummins factory, on a 500,000 sq. ft site, was designed to employ 1,250 men, turning out diesel engines.

By the 1950s Cummins engines made in Darlington were being sold and serviced in 125 countries throughout the world; and this number grew year by year. In 1964 the Cummins Darlington factory began producing two new diesel power units and that same year Chrysler International built a sturdy 'Farmobil', which combined the best features of rural utility and city delivery features. This vehicle was developed at Darlington especially for use in countries requiring low-cost transportation.

On 1 May 1965 a huge chimney was placed on the 90ft high silo at the Chrysler Cummins factory. Its purpose was to extract fumes from the engine test bed.

On 23 April 1968 the Cummins Engine Company announced that it had agreed to buy out Chrysler from their joint operation of the Chrysler Cummins assembly plant at Darlington.

In the 1970s Brooke Marine was building patrol boats for service in the West Indies. These patrol boats were powered by Cummins engines built at Darlington.

Yet all was not well at the Cummins factory site. Jobs were at risk and pickets were out. However, things soon took a turn for the better and, under the sound leadership of managing director Mr Euan MacFarlane, Cummins became one of the country's leading exporters.

On 7 September, 1982, Mr MacFarlane collected the second of two Queen's Awards for Export Achievement on behalf of Cummins Engineering Ltd. This was no mean feat.

In 1946 the Carlisle firm of John Laing and Sons began work on a contract worth well over £1 million to build a factory and administrative offices for Messrs. Patons and Baldwins Ltd, on a 140-acre site at Springfield Lane, Darlington. The contract was later extended to include an adjoining housing estate. The factory was intended to concentrate on the manufacture of hand-knitting yarn that had previously been made in mills at Halifax, Wakefield, Leicester and Melton Mowbray. It would employ about 3,000 people, a third of them men. Key workers were to be brought from the company's mills, the rest being recruited locally.

The factory covered an area of some 34 acres, the remaining 106 acres of the site being allocated to houses for key employees, an administrative block containing a training centre for operatives, lecture room, offices for the personnel manager, doctor, dentist, chiropodist, nursing staff and so on.

In 1960 Patons and Baldwins of Darlington and J. and P. Coates of Paisley, two of the leaders in the wool and cotton trades, merged. It was the richest merger in the textile industry, the two companies having between them £130 million in assets. Together they covered a combined market capital of over £106 million.

The two companies worked in harmony in the export markets and the news of this merger was unexpected in the City, although in 1959 J. and P. Coates had taken over from Patons and Baldwins a quarter-share interest in Fleming Reid, the Scotch Wool Shop group. The merger brought new importance to 'Cotton Wool' and all was well.

Kind-hearted knitters used up their oddments to make up simple tops that were donated to Oxfam and distributed all over the world; and over 50,000 third world children benefited from this unique programme.

In 1987, Mr Alistair Henderson, managing director of Patons and Baldwins was also president of the Confederation of British Wool Textiles Ltd. In 2002 the whole of the Patons and Baldwins site was controlled by Lingfield Warehouses. Patons and Baldwins stopped producing wool at Darlington but continued to run a distribution centre from the site.

At the beginning of November 1976, Carreras Rothmans confirmed that it would be taking over part of the Patons and Baldwins Darlington site and would be in production before Christmas. The announcement was made from their Basildon factory.

In 1869 Louis Rothman was born in the Ukraine. He was sent to work in his uncle's large tobacco factory near Kiev and it was there that he acquired his knowledge of tobacco and tobacco blending, which was to make him one of the world's master blenders. In 1887 he emigrated to England, aged 21 and with a capital of just £40, and founded the Rothmans business in small premises in Fleet Street. In 1900 he acquired a shop in Pall Mall, which gave its name to the famous brand of cigarettes introduced at that time to Buckingham Palace and well-known London clubs. On Louis Rothman's death in 1926, his son, Sydney, carried on the business using only the finest tobacco.

By 1977 the Darlington factory was employing about 400 people and this figure quickly rose to 1,000 as production built up to 1,000 million cigarettes a month. Most of the cigarettes produced by the Darlington factory were Rothman's King Size and were for export. Thus the famous Rothman's black cat became established in Darlington.

The unemployed of Darlington greeted Rothmans promise of 1,000 new jobs with delight. The trade unions were also delighted with the move. But established firms viewed the prospect with horror because their pay rates were pegged down by law and they feared that Rothman's higher wages would draw away the areas much-needed skilled workers. The rates of pay offered by the tobacco giant were far above those offered by many local factories.

From its early days Rothmans International took its place among the world's leading multi-national tobacco companies. Rothmans of Pall Mall (International), of which the factory at Darlington was a part, was the group's main export department. The group's most important assets were its brands and its employees. With about 17,000 employees worldwide, particular attention was given to developing and maintaining an experienced base of international managers who were well trained and highly motivated. Training courses were a feature of Rothmans Darlington factory.

On 5 June 1986, Rothmans Darlington factory produced its one hundred millionth packet of cigarettes.

Rothmans was one of the Rothmans (International) Group's three trademarks the other two being Dunhill and Stuyvesant. All three were among the top fifteen international trademarks in the world.

Stonebridge, Darlington, after Pease's Mill fire, 26 February 1894, and showing the piles driven into the River Skerne for the commencement of building the present bridge.

Pease's Mill suffered a second disastrous fire in 1933. This dramatic picture shows how the whole mill was destroyed.

A sad end to a Darlington landmark, despite hopes of conservationists that Pease's Mill would be restored as an industrial monument. The mill had suffered so much damage at the hands of vandals that it had become an unsafe eyesore. Darlington Council said it was dangerous, so it had to come down.

Erected in 1856, this bell, sited high on Pease's Mill, was taken down in November 1982 as part of the demolition of the mill.

Pease's Mill has a history going back over 200 years. Until the 1960s, its premises were also on the other side of Lower Priestgate, behind the public library, left of the picture. The mill was demolished in 1982.

Former Pease's employees Elizabeth Edwards and Irene Dawson.

A storage pressure vessel being constructed in the Whessoe factory, 1961.

A 121ft Whessoe-built storage pressure vessel negotiating the Blackwellgate/Grange Road corner at Darlington on Friday 10 April 1964.

Mr Michael Noone, a
director of Whessoe and
an authority on welding
techniques (wearing a
hat), inspecting work in
progress, April 1963.

Years ahead of their time,
Whessoe employees, in
1989, show the way to
combat global warming.

Working with a white-hot bar in Darlington and Simpson Rolling Mills, 12 August 1963.

Inside Darlington and Simpson Rolling Mills Ltd, January 1982.

The Duke of Kent's visit to
Darlington and Simpson Rolling
Mills, July 1982.

Stephen Gibson (left) and Stephen
Wright, group managers, in the
rock garden, Darlington and
Simpson Rolling Mills Ltd, in
Whessoe Road.

Cleveland Bridge's original headquarters at Smithfield Road, Darlington.

Cleveland Bridge and Engineering Co. Ltd, moving to new premises, December 1981.

Cleveland Bridge's new headquarters on Yarm Road Industrial Estate, January 1982.

Cummins Engine Company Ltd's factory is set in 30 acres of open countryside on the outskirts of Darlington and covers an area of 158,394sq. ft. The exterior walls are made of two materials: high-strength corrosion-resistant steel which, left in its natural state and unpainted, eventually turns into a rich, dark brown colour, and tinted grey glass, held in place by special neoprene gaskets. To provide a working headroom of 16ft throughout the factory, lighting, water and heating have all been suspended directly beneath the flat roof. Cummins factory is unique in the United Kingdom and proves that such a building can be architecturally exciting as well as being highly functional.

Councillor C. Spence, chairman of Darlington Development Committee (centre) and Councillor S. Oliver, vice-chairman, paying an informal visit to Chrysler Cummins Ltd, Darlington on 25 March 1965.

Mr Euan McFarland, director of Cummins Ltd, Darlington, pictured here in March 1982. That year Cummins won the Queen's Award for Export Achievements.

Mr Derek Harnby with an
engine built by Cummins
on show at Bondgate
Memorial Hall, Darlington.

Patons and Baldwins lorries
carrying part of a consignment
of 170 metric tons of machine
knitting yarn, destined for an
iron curtain country on 29
September 1967. They are
pictured at the Patons factory in
Darlington leaving for the
Surrey Dock in London. The
complete shipment represents
the firm's biggest export
consignment and had been
produced by a concerted effort
on the part of Patons' factories
in the North East.

Patons and Baldwins sales
managers from nearly
every country in Western
Europe look over the goods
at the firm's factory at
Darlington, where they are
attending an annual
conference, March 1969.

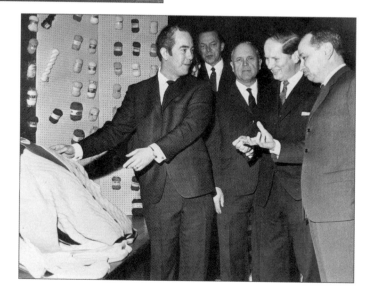

Patons and Baldwins put on a fashion show for Marks & Spencer, 25 September 1970.

Over 50,000 Third World children benefited from a unique scheme started by Patons and Baldwins when kind-hearted knitters used up their wool and oddments to make simple tops. These were donated to Oxfam and distributed all over the world.

Patons' locomotive, now in North Road Railway Museum.

Flying the flag, Councillor Bill Newton helps Rothmans celebrate record sales abroad, 25 April 1985.

Michael Allison MP (left), Minister of State for Employment, inspect top-quality tobacco used in the manufacture of Rothmans cigarettes.

Tony Blair, MP for Sedgefield (second right), being handed a petition against tobacco tax by Rothmans personnel, 4 January 1985.

Ann Jopling, Rothmans packer, with the 1,000 millionth packet of cigarettes produced at the Darlington factory.

4 *Darlington Growing*

During Darlington's years as a market town, it was approached along broad roads. During the first half of the nineteenth century, many handsome villas were built on the approaches to Darlington, set back from the town's approach roads. They were set in tastefully laid-out grounds, backed by gardens and orchards which exuded prosperity.

Darlington's most influential families occupied these villas. They were the families which had been in the forefront of the town's industrial development; foremost among them the Peases, the Backhouses and the Whitwells. Only one of these villas was situated on the left side of the River Skerne. It was Eastmount, built for John Pease, (1797–1868), the eldest son of Edward Pease. Its long gardens spread down to the Skerne and were joined to the gardens of Edward Pease's house in Northgate by a footbridge.

Of all the Darlington villas, Pierremont, erected in the 1830s, was unusual because it was built of stone in the Gothic style. It belonged to John Botcherby of Beechwood, but most of the Darlington villas had Backhouse connections.

The less affluent lived in newly built terraces. As Darlington's population increased, houses were built in the gardens of the villas closest to the town and the original owners moved further out.

New terraces were built on Northgate, Coniscliffe Lane and Harewood Hill and Grove. These were occupied by poorer Darlingtonians. Streets of more modest houses appeared and spread out, mainly north of Bondgate. Darlington Gas Light Company was formed on 25 November 1830, with over forty shareholders. It provided 150 gaslights in the main streets, the gas coming from their gas works, sited slightly south of the Stockton & Darlington Railway. A lamplighter was employed to turn the lights on and off between 1 September and 1 May, except for the three nights before and two nights after each full moon, unless the nights were very dark.

POSTAL SERVICES

Darlington's first post office was in Charegate, which was sometimes called Glover's Weind and is known today as Post House Wynd. It was later transferred to the corner of Old Post office Yard now known as Buckton's Yard and High Row.

Until 1784 horse-mounted post boys carried the mail. Then Prime Minister William Pitt allowed stage coaches to carry the post, protected by an armed guard. This resulted in letters being carried more quickly and more securely than with the post boys. The postal cost was still paid by the receiver and was still charged on weight and the distance carried. Then, in 1840, the penny post was introduced and the sender bore the cost.

By 1840, Darlington Post Office had moved to Northgate, but the premises were demolished to make way for the entrance to Crown Street, which was in the process of being built. The post office reopened a few yards further south in 1865. Today it occupies a prime site on St Cuthbert's Way.

WATER SUPPLY

Before 1850, most Darlingtonians relied on nineteen public and about four hundred private wells for their water supply, which was taken from the wells by pump or buckets. This was not satisfactory because water seeped back into the wells and polluted them.

On 28 April 1850, the Tees Cottage Water Works opened, controlled by the Darlington Gas and Water Company. This event caused much local rejoicing. The bells of St Cuthbert's and St John's churches rang out, a brass band played in the Central Hall, a 100ft jet of water cascaded into the Market Square and celebratory feasts were eaten in the Sun Inn and the King's Head.

Darlington Gas and Water Company lost no time in pumping water from the River Tees and passing it through settling beds with sand filters before pumping it on to Bushel Hill reservoir, which had been built to hold 800,000 gallons.

The Darlington Gas and Water Company laid down stringent conditions for the plumbing work in the buildings supplied with its water.

A scale of quarterly charges to be paid in advance, was drawn up for domestic dwellings with price variations for dwellings that were part shops or buildings that were complete shops. Water for horses and cattle had special rates. Darlington Gas and Water Company was sold to the Darlington Board of Health in 1854.

FIRE SERVICE

Darlington's first firefighting equipment consisted of leather buckets for holding water to throw on the fire, ladles for throwing soil and mud onto it and ropes and fire hooks, which were used to pull down burning thatch and unsafe walls. Most of this equipment was kept in St Cuthbert's church. None of it was of much use against a very ferocious fire like the one that damaged the woollen factory belonging to Edward and Joseph Pease in February 1817, and cost more than 500 employees their jobs.

A meeting was held early in 1837 to discuss the prevention and lighting of fires and there it was agreed to hold a public subscription for the purchase of a manual fire pump, a water tank on wheels from which water was pumped by hand into a flexible hose from where it was directed by a line of men with buckets. The fire pump was housed in Park Street.

In 1850 a Superintendent of the Fire Brigade was appointed at £3 10s per annum. He was responsible for the maintenance of equipment and had twelve firemen under him. The firemen were paid 2s for attending a practice every quarter with extra payment for attending fires.

That same year George Mason, surveyor to the Town Commissioners, tried to dispense with the firemen as an economic measure, leaving only the superintendent and himself. Bystanders would be asked to help in the event of a fire. They would be paid 1s for the first hour and 6d for each subsequent hour. George Mason's suggestion was not carried out.

At a meeting held in November 1850 between the local agents of various insurance societies on the one hand and Messrs T.M. Cockin, John Pease, John Beaumont Pease and Robert Thompson on the other, it was agreed to hand over the subscription fire engine to the Darlington Board of Health, 'provided it was kept in efficient working order and that an efficient Fire Brigade was formed.' The provisions were carried out and from these beginnings the fire brigade has developed into the efficient fire service Darlington has today.

ON THE MOVE

The Great North Road, the principal route between London and Edinburgh, passed through Darlington; and that section of it between Borough Bridge and Durham was turnpiked. The turnpike company collecting the tolls from passengers undertook to maintain their section of the road in reasonable condition.

The Great North Road, was one of several turnpike roads in the Darlington area that developed around the mid-eighteenth century. Carriers used them for the conveyance of passengers and parcels to the surrounding villages and further afield, going as far as Kendal. The carriages were all horse-drawn.

By the 1880s, horse-drawn trams were operating throughout Darlington. At each terminus, the two horses pulling the single-decker trams were disconnected and moved to the rear of the vehicle where they were reconnected, ready for the return journey. By about 1900, both single-decker and double-decker trams were in regular use.

In about 1903 tramlines were laid along Darlington's main streets and in June 1904, Mrs Henderson, the Mayoress of Darlington opened the Darlington Corporation Light Railway. This marked the end of an era for horse-drawn trams. In 1914, trams came into use that gave some protection to the driver from the weather. The Darlington Corporation Light Railway lasted until 1926.

By the late 1940s traffic in Darlington had increased dramatically. The nose-to-tail situation was becoming commonplace. Trolleybuses and buses ferried passengers throughout the town and police were on point duty at busy corners like the ones at Blackwell and Skinnergate and High Row and Horsemarket. In the Leadyard, sited south of St Cuthbert's churchyard and so named because lead belonging to the Bishop of Durham was stored there, was the town's bus station for all except the corporation services. It was a situation that would get worse before it got better.

EDUCATION

In Darlington formal education began at St Cuthbert's church in about 1530 when the priest of the newly founded chantry of All Saints in St Cuthbert's church was required to keep 'a free School of Grammar for all manner of children thither resorting.'

In 1547, when chantries were abolished, the school was allowed to continue under a Royal warrant. In 1563, a petition from the people of Darlington to Queen Elizabeth I resulted in the re-endowment of the school with the lands and properties that had once supported the chantry.

Until 1813, the schoolhouse stood between the east end of St Cuthbert's and the River Skerne. But lack of burial space caused wardens to order the school's demolition. A single-storey replacement was built at the eastern end of the Leadyard near a footbridge over the Skerne. In 1846 a second storey was added to the building.

For many years the free Grammar School struggled with financial troubles and mediocre teachers, some of whom supplemented their income by taking private boarding pupils and adding extra subjects for which fees could be charged.

By 1845 the sad state of the grammar school was brought to the attention of the people of Darlington by one of the governors. The headmaster, the Revd George Wray, was blamed for all the school's troubles, but he refused to leave the schoolhouse or hand over the keys. The school governors had been trying to get rid of the Revd Wray for five years and were determined that this was the time for him to go. By now there were only about a dozen scholars in the school and alternative accommodation had to be found for them. First they used a small room in Houndgate, then one in Skinnergate.

In the lengthy and expensive lawsuit that followed, the Revd Wray claimed that he had been unfairly dismissed while the governors argued that he had been guilty of negligence. The Revd Wray won his case, which was heard at Durham, but the governors appealed to the Court of Queen's Bench and the original decision was overturned. Then at a further appeal to the Lord Chief Justice and other judges the appeal was upheld.

The Revd John Marshall succeeded Wray and stayed with the school until he retired in 1875. During that time the school continued to receive criticism. In 1874 the grammar school received a new charter under the Endowed Schools Act of 1869 and, in 1879, moved to new premises in Vane Terrace, designed by G.G. Hoskins. One unusual feature of the building was a covered play area beneath the main hall. However, lack of space saw this converted into a laboratory.

In February 1872, the British and Foreign Schools Society opened its North of England College for Training Mistresses for Elementary Schools in Darlington. Initially, thirty-eight students were trained there. Within three years numbers had almost doubled and an adjoining house had to be leased to accommodate them. In 1917, the College established a nursery school in North Lodge Terrace for training nursery teachers and in 1918 Fairfield in Woodland Road was acquired with financial help from J.M. Dent, the Darlington-born publisher. It was named George Dent Nursery School in memory of J.M. Dent's father.

In the nineteenth century, Darlington was well endowed with private schools, there being fifteen in the 1828/9 school year. Polam Hall, an independent school for girls was one of them. It originated in the school for the education of the daughters of Quakers families in Selby House, Houndgate, in 1848, by three sisters, Jane, Barbara and Elizabeth Proctor. Ten years later the school moved to Polam Hall, the former home of Jonathan Backhouse. When Jane Proctor died in 1882, the school's fortune became uncertain and it closed in 1887. Then, in 1888, Hannah and Rachel Lockwood moved their existing girls' school from Kendal to Darlington and reopened Polam Hall with eleven pupils. Today Polam Hall is a very successful school.

RELIGIOUS DARLINGTON

St Cuthbert's is the Parish Church of Darlington and it stands on or near a much earlier church that existed early in the eleventh century. Between 1003 and 1036, an influential Danish noble gave lands including 'Dearnington.' (Darlington), to the Episcopal See of Durham 'for St Cuthbert.'

Danish invasions followed and William the Conqueror's invasion of the North in 1069 and raids by Malcolm of Scotland in 1072 came quickly after that. It is very unlikely that the small church survived all these onslaughts. By 1080 there was probably no church there at all.

However, during the episcopate of William of Calais, a Norman church was constructed there. In 1083 secular or married priests were displaced for the Benedictine Priory of Durham and homes were found for then, many in Darlington. It was at this time that St Cuthbert's was elevated to a collegiate church, which meant that it now supported a vicar and four prebends, whose stipends came from various parts of the parish. This comprised Darlington, Blackwell, Cockerton and Archdeacon Newton.

The larger church of Bishop Puiset superseded the small Norman church and although the parish of Darlington covered a large area, it did not warrant a church as large as the one which Bishop Puiset envisaged. To him, Darlington had a special significance because it now had the right to hold markets and fairs, so a large church was fitting. Bishop Puiset built a manor house or Bishop's Palace near the south side of the churchyard. It was demolished in 1870 and the present Town Hall occupies the site.

In 1439, Richard Wytton, then vicar of St Cuthbert's church, complained about his low status to Bishop Neville and the bishop raised him to Dean. His Deanery occupied what is now the Dolphin Centre.

In 1547 the collegiate church was dissolved and St Cuthbert's again became a parish church with a vicar and a curate. The bishop remained the Lord of the Manor and the chief citizen was his bailiff. It was not until 1876 that Darlington had an elected mayor. For this reason Darlington had no great local families with family pews, private chapels, commemorative stained-glass windows or magnificent tombs. So St Cuthbert's church became unusual in that, despite its undistinguished history, it was more written about and illustrated than any other church in the parish.

Although St Cuthbert's is Darlington Parish Church, the Society of Friends, the Quakers, is so strongly associated with the town that Darlington Football Club is nicknamed the Quakers.

In about 1850, when Darlington's population was around 11,500 people, several religious establishments served the town. There were four Methodist chapels, a Baptist chapel, a Bethel Independent chapel, three Anglican churches, a Roman Catholic church and a Friends Meeting House. Had every Darlingtonian been a regular worshipper, collectively these places of worship would not have been able to cope.

Today with Darlington's population around 100,000, and with roughly the same number of places of worship as there were 150 years ago, these, with rare exceptions like the C of E Church of St James the Great, are emptier than they used to be 150 years ago.

BANKING

The Backhouses and the Peases were both distinguished and established family dynasties. When they came to Darlington in the mid-eighteenth century, they worked first in linens and woollens, moving later into railways, coal mining, ironstone mining, quarrying, brick-making and water supply. In so doing they became very wealthy. They strove for educational and social welfare in and around Darlington. The Backhouses went into banking in a big way. In 1774 James Backhouse and his son, Jonathan, together founded Backhouse's Bank in Northgate. Later they moved the bank to High Row. As the bank became established, branches and agencies were opened in the main towns of the region. In 1896, when Backhouses Bank merged with Barclay and Co. to form Barclay's Bank, all seventeen of its partners were Backhouses. The last Backhouse partner served Barclays Bank until 1973.

The first £5 note issued by Backhouse's Darlington Bank showed the year in which the bank was founded, 1774, and a sketch of St Cuthbert's church and the old three-arched bridge over the River Skerne. All Backhouse Bank's £5 notes were dated in the Quaker way, like this: '12th of the 4th month, 1864.'

In 1910 the London City and Midland Bank erected a splendid building on the corner of High Row and Bondgate. In 1923 the bank moved to new premises across the road in Prospect Place and Pearl Assurance took over the vacated building. The bank remains at No. 1 Prospect Place under its new name HSBC.

Today seven banks look after the financial interests of Darlington and its inhabitants.

DARLINGTON PUBLIC LIBRARY

In 1793, Darlington Public Library was instituted and housed in part of the Central Buildings. Membership was £2 12s 6d and 10s 6d annually. This put the library beyond the reach of working men and women. Because Darlington now had a subscription library, much opposition was met by many Quakers who began lobbying for a public library. An added charge on the rates was another reason for opposing a public library. But the opposition diminished when Edward Pease left £10,000 to build and equip a public library. In 1933 the library was extended by the Borough Architect. He used the same brick, stone and decoration so, like Ernie Wise's wig, it was almost impossible to see the join. Down the years Darlington Public Library in Crown Street, has proved its worth time and time again. Today it continues to play an integral part in the life of Darlington and is a town treasure.

LAW AND ORDER

In about 1800, Darlington had two unpaid police constables to maintain law and order, with many of the local land and property owners standing together to form a private Association for the Prosecution of Felons. Then, in January 1822, a meeting of the interested Darlingtonians resolved to put a stop to the rowdiness, which for so long had prevailed in the town. The intention was good, but nothing came of it.

In 1808 the magistrates of Darlington rented a large room in the Town Hall for use as a court room. On 24 August 1846 Darlington got its first police station and court room, financed partly by county rates and in part by subscription. That same year the town's first police station was built in Grange Road. It was staffed by a superintendent, two sergeants and seventeen constables.

Industrial development to the north of the town during the 1860s caused many disturbances and breaches of the peace, as a result of which the police had the unenviable task of having to march offenders through the town centre to the police station. So a new, more conveniently sited police station was built on the corner of Northgate and Chestnut Street in 1868. The police station is now sited on St Cuthbert's Way. It has been there since 1964.

HEALTH

Darlington has been a prime mover in public health since the middle of the nineteenth century and was deeply involved in the transfer of welfare from workhouse to welfare state. Darlington workhouse, known as Easthaven, and now demolished, had a hospital for the very elderly and sick.

Darlington water works.

Gunpowder explosion at
J.F. Smythe's, gunsmiths,
10 October 1894.

Binns blaze, 1925. The fireman on the ladder is using a hose to extinguish the flames.

Bondgate, c. 1890. At this time horse power denoted the strength of the horse pulling the gig.

No room for vehicles here, First World War volunteers crowd the Blackwellgate/Skinnergate corner as the Union flag they serve flies proudly.

It is 1925 and a car makes a comeback. The man on the roof is playing safe.

St Cuthbert's church (in the background, right), towers over a cavalcade of conveyances passing Darlington's open market on the left in the early 1930s.

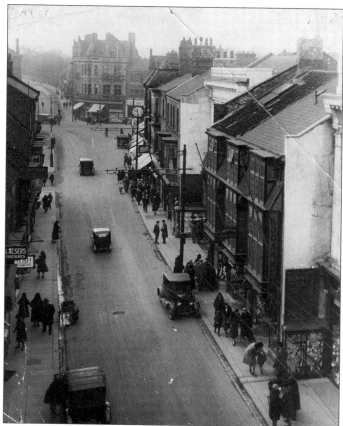

Blackwellgate in 1934 when traffic did not cause the problems it does today. What a refreshing scene.

Skinnergate, 1936. Two types of horsepower meet.

It is 1964 and girls working in Baum's of Bondgate are terrified that vehicles going up Commercial Street will bring the shop crushing about their ears.

On 25 November 1965, this bus met the wrong type of snow lying all of one inch deep on Victoria Road. It could not cope so the passengers got out and pushed.

This policeman in Blackwellgate is reading the riot act to the driver of the Morris 1000. The lady driver in the car behind can't understand why, 24 June 1974.

A 1930s classroom in Dodmire Junior School, decorated to celebrate the school's Golden Jubilee.

Dodmire Infant School pupils Corinna Bagnall and Mark Rowe concentrate on their writing on 27 May 1987. Phew!

Three Dodmire School infants, 26 February 1986, painting egg holders and showing exquisite taste in reading material.

St Cuthbert's church with the post-Reformation grammar school building on the right.

St Cuthbert's church from the west, 1843. The west door, a feature generally found in collegiate churches, can be clearly seen.

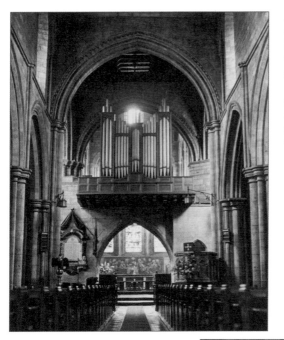

A view down the nave of St Cuthbert's church. In 1899 lead from the tower was lifted and it was found that a tower top was covered with medieval gravestones and that the spire, weighing at least 150 tons, had been built on them. This caused the tower to settle by at least 20cm. This was why the windows and arching north and south in the transept were blocked as the picture shows.

The vicar of St Cuthbert's addressing a special women's day, World of Prayer service in February 1975.

Six of St Cuthbert's church bells in 1937, awaiting transportation to be recast to mark the coronation of King George VI. The largest, the tenor bell, weighs over 16 cwt. The one on the extreme right is dated 1755.

Midland Bank, No. 1
Prospect Place,
Darlington,
27 November 1974.

Midland Bank Coat of Arms, 1961.

Cockerton branch of
the Midland Bank in
1966, was taking no
chances of being
broken into – it was
on wheels!

Speedy Westminster Bank, Darlington, 10 August 1961.

Lloyds new bank, Cockerton, Darlington, 24 November 1967.

First customer, Mr Arnold Hadwin, editor of the *Evening Despatch*, gets £10 from the newly installed cash dispenser at the National Provincial Bank, High Row, 27 November 1969. Customers could get instant cash if they had a special computerised card to operate the machine. Looking on (left to right) are Mr R.L. Stockdale, manager National Bank, Mr D.A. Howkin, manager Westminster Bank and Mr G.B. Peck, manager District Bank.

Barclays Bank, High Row, Darlington, 11 May 1993.

Bank clerks Denise Jolly and Jean Burluraux with sub-manager Stanley Harrison, look as though they have been well trained. Pictured here on 2 May 1975, they are on the right lines with Nat West.

Lloyds Bank, Skinnergate branch. In 1992 it was the scene of a raid.

The smiling manager and staff of Yorkshire Bank, Darlington branch, offer a sincere and warm welcome to current and potential customers on 13 May 1993.

5 On The Town

A SHOPPING EXPERIENCE

Darlington's main shopping areas fall into two distinct parts, Ancient and Modern. The town's ancient open market, which is more than 400 years old, shares its antiquity with High Row, possibly the oldest inhabited area in the Borough of Darlington.

High Row lies across the brow of a one-time, east-facing grassy slope where early sun worshippers erected their crude huts to face the rising sun. For many years the open market occupied the broad expanse of land that spread westwards from the entrance to St Cuthbert's Church to the bottom of the grassy bank along the top of which High Row lay.

Until the mid-nineteenth century, the Bishop of Durham (and afterwards the Ecclesiastical Commissioners), owned Darlington's market place, its street end polls, the highways in the town, the Town Hall and the shambles. In 1853, the town's polls owners considered plans for a butter and egg market building, but nothing came of the project. On 16 May 1856, an agreement was reached by which, on payment of £7,885 the Board of Health in Darlington became the owner of all the above that had originally belonged to the Bishop of Durham and payment of tolls was abolished.

In 1860 the Board of Health offered a premium of £100 for the best design for a large market hall and offices. Many plans were submitted but the board could not agree as to which design was the best one to use, and engaged Mr Waterhouse, a well-known architect, to draw up a scheme incorporating the best features of the designs sent in. The estimated cost of £14,000 was considered exorbitant at first and many local people objected to having a large building in the market place.

On 7 August 1862 the objectors presented a memorial to the Board of Health condemning the market hall scheme but they were informed that the contract had been signed for the work to go ahead. The building of the market hall and the offices was completed in 1863.

Darlington had been very busy market town for hundreds of years, with open stalls in the market place where all sorts of foodstuffs were displayed for sale, often soiled with grime and soot from the nearby factories. On 2 May 1864, the market hall was opened for business, the first purchase being made by Mr J. Wrightson, landlord of the Sun Inn, who bought a large leg of mutton.

It was early in 1864 that the clock tower was added to the market hall on the suggestion of Mr Joseph Pease, who had seen and admired a similar tower on one of his Continental tours. Mr Pease also gave the clock with its four 7ft dials and the five clock bells. When the bells were delivered in 1864 it was found that the two smallest bells were unsuitable for the belfry. They were later given to St Cuthbert's Church to make up its peal of bells and were first hung there to celebrate Mr Pease's 67th birthday on 22 June 1866. The market clock bells were first heard in the town at 3.30pm on 3 July 1864, when the inhabitants heard the strains from their own sweet chiming bells.

The open arcades on the north and east sides of the market hall were added in 1866 at an additional cost of £2,611.

During the following year, 1867, a Charter of Incorporation was granted by Queen Victoria, which greatly enhanced the civic dignity of the borough, and in 1915 Darlington obtained the status of County Borough – a new prestige and new responsibilities were wisely encouraged and undertaken by the local government authorities.

Many years before the market hall was built, Dame Dorothy Brown, a descendent of Richard Barns, Bishop of Durham, erected a market cross to replace an earlier one, which had crumbled away through old age. She did this in 1727 and the market cross was sited slightly north of where the clock tower now stands.

The market cross is of Roman design and its emblem shape represents peace and security. It originally had three steps and stood on a square pedestal, the pillar being round, surmounted by a ball at the top. It was always the custom in Darlington for a cortège to rest at the foot of the market cross before proceeding to a burial ceremony at nearby St Cuthbert's Church. The market cross has since been re-sited at the west end of Houndgate.

For more than 400 years the open market has worked on Saturdays as well as Mondays, both days being equally busy. It was also open on some Bank Holidays when other nearby town centre shops were closed. But it was more than that. Mr Charlie Hall, a wonderful character, whose heartwarming spiel was an absolute joy, used to say, 'This is the oldest business in the town and it really is Darlington's village green.'

Charlie was not allowed to sell cut flowers so he sold bulbs from Holland and Spalding. He added humour to his sales patter, like on the occasion when a prospective lady customer spent some time inspecting his tulip bulbs: 'What is the difference between those marked nine pence and those marked twelve pence?' she asked. Quick as a flash, Charlie replied, 'Three pence.'

On another occasion a lady called Gladys came into the covered market to buy some biscuits from a stall opposite Charlie's. She fell backwards over a biscuit tin, into Charlie's arms. It was a case of love at first sight and later they married.

Another stallholder, Percy Pigg, had probably the loudest voice in all the market. So deafening was it that the local authority had to tell him to be less noisy.

Jack Gowland's method of attracting a crowd was quite different. He wore a wig and a mask, and it worked.

Other stallholders did not resort to such extreme methods, but each had his or her own individual gimmick. One lady with a greengrocery stall so enjoyed the fruit and vegetables she sold that there were times when her profit margin suffered.

Many of the businesses in both the covered and the open markets have been long established. It was with much pride that businesses passed from one generation to another down the same family.

Throughout the market, the owner of a butchery business was called a master butcher. But a butcher employed by the master butcher could not call himself a master butcher, even though he may have been as skilled as the butcher for whom he worked. He was a journeyman butcher and would not become a master butcher until he owned his own butchering business.

One of the meat stalls in the covered market is owned by David Beck who, when he started as a fifteen-year-old apprentice, had to watch calves being killed. 'It was a stomach-churning experience,' he said, 'but you get used to it.'

During the depression of the 1930s, when there was no heating in the covered market, vegetables often froze to the stall; and, although stall rents were only 2s 6d a week, it was difficult to make a living. Indeed, it was a happy day if a stallholder made £2 on a Saturday.

In those days the covered market closed at 8.30pm on Saturday nights. This was the time of day when regular crowds of Darlington housewives converged on the vegetable stalls, eager to grab discarded produce for next to nothing. Many a Sunday roast was enhanced in this way.

One stallholder who sold bacon, had various ways of keeping shoppers entertained. One day he brought an entire band of travelling musicians into the covered market and on another occasion he brought a donkey into the market, much to the delight of the youngsters.

Ernie Barnett devoted a large part of his working life to helping fellow stallholders to stand up and fight for their rights. Always a talker, he also enjoyed getting things done. He was founder chairman of the Market Stallholders' Association, which began from an initial meeting in Paradise Hall, Coniscliffe Road, Darlington. He was also an active member of the Darlington Pensioners' Association and is justly proud of helping to achieve higher pension rights for them.

Ernie's father came from Newcastle and opened up a stall in the covered market selling fruit, trays of toffee, eucalyptus soap and, the best bargain of all, two packets of Woodbines with a box of matches for 2½d.

Speaking for all the stallholders, Ernie reminds us that people will always want fresh produce, rather than pre-packed food. The big firms forget that people might like to buy just one apple and not the four they often have to buy when they are wrapped up before sale.

Long-established businesses and relative newcomers to the covered market tend to work alongside one another in harmony. Audrey Snowdon had always liked the market's atmosphere and thought she could do well with a stall, even though she had never worked in a market.

One hundred years ago, Mr Blair established a successful business in the covered market, which his grandson, Robin Blair, runs so well. He succinctly sums up the work of both the covered and open markets like this: 'All stallholders want to do is to make an honest living.'

One trader who did not have a stall was Mr D. Luca, who for many years had a tea bar under the canopy of the covered market. He also had, in the mid-1930s, an ice cream factory in Bondgate and a fleet of ice cream carts. The jackets and aprons worn by his salesmen were all dazzling white.

During 1978–9 the covered market was refurbished and a new flagged floor was laid. So it became even more attractive to shoppers while still retaining its old world charm. This exciting development was given an award by the Civic Trust.

SLAUGHTERHOUSE STREETS

In the sixteenth century, a row of stalls was placed in the shambles, sited at the south-western corner of what is now the covered market. They were for the exclusive use of those stall holders who dealt in meat and fish. It was not a very salubrious area because the butchers invariably failed to clear up the excessive amount of blood, entails and offal – leftovers of the cattle slaughtered there. This led to much friction between the butchers and the local authority.

Market day was held on Mondays with fair days for the sale of horned cattle and sheep being held on alternative Mondays from Whit Monday until Christmas. Special fair days or Great Mondays, were held throughout the year. The sale of cattle was exempted from tolls at these Great Monday sales. Horses and pigs were sold on special days during November.

Farm workers and servants were hired for six-monthly periods and the Mondays before and after May Day and Martinmass were hiring days. Since most prospective employers paid roughly the same wage, other considerations had to be taken into account. One frequent question was. 'Is it a good grub shop?'

In 1736, one of the offences heard by the Darlington Court concerned a Darlington victualler called Robert Coates, who was accused of allowing his pigs to roam around the streets unheeded 'to the greatest hindrance of the people and our sovereign, the King. Therefore he is at the mercy of the Lord. Fined 5/-.'

Court appearances did not make much difference to the sad state of Darlington's mid-town streets so, on 29 October 1788, the following vestry order was introduced:

At a public meeting held this day in the Vestry pursuant to notice given for taking into consideration the cleaning of the streets of Darlington and appointing a Scavenger for that purpose, we whose names are hereunto subscribed, are of the opinion that the same is highly requisite and that the manure scraped therefrom may be turned to an advantage and let for an annual sum which is to be appropriated to the necessary repairs of the said streets and Highways and Richard Fawcett now attending this meeting and offering to give the Annual some of Eight pounds for such manure: It is unanimously agreed to accept the said offer and nominate him Scavenger for that purpose which is agreed accordingly. And Mr. Weatherall, of Field House has assumed and pretends to have an exclusive right to the Manure bred in all the said streets of the said Town that none also aught to take the same. It is agree that in case the said Mr. Wetherall shall persist in such right or bring any Action at Law for establishing the same, that the said Action shall be defended at the expense of the Town and that Mr. Arman shall defend same.

After Darlington Council opened a cattle mart at Clifton Row in 1878, the sale of livestock in the centre of the town declined. But for many more years flocks of geese, en route to the new market, were rested on High Row. It was not until 1914 that Bondgate ceased to be a market for sheeptrading.

SHOPS & SERVICES

High Row is the birthplace of industry and commerce in Darlington. It was there that, in the early nineteenth century, several small banks were established, two of which developed through the Backhouse and Pease textile interests. All the banks had the ability to advance credit to customers and to receive it from suppliers and this enabled both businesses to thrive.

High Row has always been one of the most important façades in Darlington. Flags front this long row of fine buildings, divided mid-way along it by Post House Wynd, and east of the flags, the land fell away to meet the Great North Road below, as it edges the covered market.

In Tudor times cobble paving was preferable to the deep mud it replaced and that was why the hillside fronting High Row was cobbled. At the beginning of the eighteenth century, the cobbles were repaired, many being replaced. In 1901, Darlington Council removed all the cobbles.

Until 1914, when sheep were finally removed from the slope, it was topped with a row of posts and chains to prevent animals wandering onto the flagged path fronting the buildings along the bank top.

Flanking the Great North Road that entered Darlington via Blackwellgate and headed for Scotland via Northgate, both High Row and Prebend Row now provided a wide variety of shops and services that caters for the residents and those who visit at any time of year.

From High Row there are fifteen entries into yards in which, in about 1850, people lived in crowded and dirty conditions. Some yards led into Skinnergate, while others led nowhere.

Post House Wynd is a busy lane that runs from High Row to Skinnergate. Its original name was Glover's Lane, but this was changed to Post House Wynd when a posthouse, the Talbot Inn, was sited there.

George Fox founded the Society of Friends, the Quakers, in the 1650s and in 1666, a small group became established in Darlington. At first they met in various private houses but, following the passing of the Act of Tolerance in 1689, the

Quakers were able to follow their religion without fear of persecution. They used two meeting houses at the south end of Skinnergate as regular places of worship.

A tree once grew at the south end of Skinnergate and an adjacent inn was named after it. When the inn became a café, the café took on the name. When the tree died, a replacement was named the Green Tree. It still stands there today.

Skinnergate has for a long while been lined with shops where the needs of customers are paramount. In about 1900, Davison's cake shop sold biscuits loose from tins, satisfying each individual customer's needs.

In 1905 Presland's hairdressing salon opened at 83 Skinnergate. Twenty years later, in 1925, it moved to 77 Skinnergate. Advertising their new location, Presland's declared that they were 'the finest Hairdressing Saloon [their spelling] in the North.' In 1957 another hairdresser, John Hunter, acquired Presland's business.

Presland's original salon became part of Bainbridge Barker's department store at the corner of Skinnergate and Blackwellgate.

Until 1843, Darlington had only two cemeteries, the principal one being at St Cuthbert's Church and the other one, a Quaker cemetery situated at Skinnergate. In 1858 the average numbers of Quakers buried in the Quaker cemetery was five per annum. All the Quaker headstones are of the same height and design because 'in the eyes of God, all people are equal.'

INN AND AROUND CENTRAL DARLINGTON

The King's Head, Prospect Place, was probably the first public house in Darlington. It was in existence in 1661 when Sir John Lowther bought it. From 1770 it was a coaching stop for the London to Newcastle post coach, the last of which ceased to run in 1852. The King's Head was then demolished, to be replaced by the present hotel, which was opened in June 1893. By the early eighteenth century, other inns had been built, including the Black Swan. Seven inns were sited on the west side of Skinnergate, but its eastern side had none.

Every hostelry advertised conveniences like a pump, brew house and stabling. When landlord John Williamson moved from the Cross Keys to the Black Swan in November 1700, he let it be known that he had 'a commodious, good house, situated in the same town, where all gentlemen travellers shall be kindly received and entertained by John Williamson.'

During the eighteenth century, Darlington's principal inns were the Swan Inn, Prospect Place, which was the only one with a room large enough to accommodate large gatherings; the Black Bull on the corner of Blackwellgate and Grange Road, known as the Bull; the Boot and Shoe in Tubwell Row, facing the market, and the Talbot at the corner of High Row and Post House Wynd. Its sign was a Talbot hunting dog with its tongue sticking out. In time, the tongue, rusted and one windy day a strong wind snapped it off, giving rise to the saying that 'Darlington wind is so strong that it once blew out a dog's tongue.'

The best place for researching Darlington's pubs is in Darlington's pubs. The longer the time spent researching the more indistinct the result. It's enough to drive a researcher to drink!

Darlington market place from the Talbot Inn, High Row, December 1845. The market cross is shown on its original site at the western end of Tubwell Row. St Cuthbert's Church is seen in the middle distance.

Tubwell Row looking towards stone bridge, c. 1890. The covered market is at the right-hand side of the picture, and many of the buildings still stand today, though much altered in appearance and purpose.

In 1727 Dame Dorothy Brown had this market cross erected to replace an earlier one, which had crumbled away owing to old age.

Darlington open market, 30 August 1965.

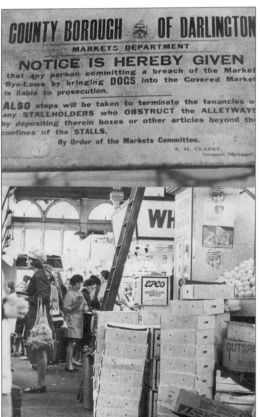

A Borough of Darlington Markets Department notice regarding breaking the Market Byelaws, pictured in 1973.

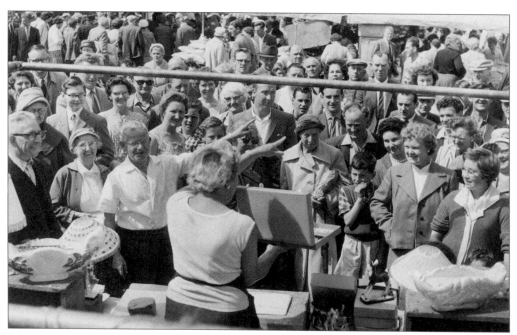

'It's a bargain at £40. But I'm not going to ask £40 for it – or £30. Not even £20. I could give it away for £10 but I'm not going to do that. It's yours for a fiver. Sold to the man over there with a smile on his face. Here you are, sir, you've got yourself a bargain.'

Sam Moore's fish stall in the covered market. His produce was always of the finest quality.

Smiling pair Allene Norris and Yvonne Talbot, outside the covered market, the subject of a book they wrote and illustrated together, September 1986.

Florist stallholder Charlie Hall, pictured in February 1980. He reluctantly gave up in 1981 after nearly forty years in the business. Much admired and greatly loved, Charlie, along with fruit and vegetable stallholders, helped to found the Market Retail Stallholders' Association.

Mr Marsh fronting his well-stocked stall.

Robin Blair's displays are always magnificent, his prices never unreasonable and nothing is sold in pre-packed multiples, so customers can buy just what they need. Needless to say it is all in season and fresh.

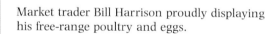
Market trader Bill Harrison proudly displaying his free-range poultry and eggs.

The Market Cross now stands at the west end of Blackwellgate. The building on the left is the old Town Hall. The spire of St Cuthbert's Church is in the middle distance.

Cattle on High Row awaiting slaughter.

Darlington cattle mart, Clifton Row, opened in 1878.

Farmers at
Darlington Auction
Mart weighing up
the beast's form
before bidding,
25 May 1964.

Sheep being auctioned at Darlington
Mart on 25 May 1964. The auctioneer
stands on the ramp, centre.

A fine bull being paraded
at Darlington Mart on
15 January 1978. He's
not there for a short time.
He's there for heifer and
heifer.

Blackwellgate in 1848.

The Green Tree Inn with its 'Good Stabling' sign prominently displayed, *c.* 1925. There is an advert for Lillian Gish's new film on the wall. A complimentary ticket to see *The White Sister* for the landlord!

High Row, *c*. 1890. The statue on the left, erected in 1875, is of Joseph Pease, (1799–1872), the first ever Quaker MP. The King's Head dominates the scene.

High Row, *c*. 1900. Here we can see the gentle slope on which the cattle market was held.

Thought by many to have been the most customer-friendly shop in Darlington, Dressers was built on the site of a pub. Throughout its life Dressers occupied two sites on High Row. The one shown here is the original site. Miss Lofthouse, who so ably managed Dressers' book department, had the rare gift of making customers feel they were the most important people in the world.

Planting a replacement tree in front of the Green Tree café, originally the Green Tree Inn, on 20 October 1965. Today's ecologically-minded people will smile on this move.

In 1991 High Row traffic was flowing along what was originally a slope. This has been replaced with a long row of four steps.

Boyes it may be but it seems to be girls who mainly shop there.

Buckton Yard, pictured on
20 October, 1975. Its gas lamp
is more in keeping with its
surroundings than the modern
electric light that front the
central gable end.

A new surface for Posthouse
Wynd, February 1986.

6   A Newspaper Town At Leisure

THE NORTHERN ECHO

When a group of far-sighted businessmen decided that the time was ripe for a radical morning paper, they chose Darlington as the headquarters of their new venture. This was because of its excellent railway facilities that allowed a newspaper printed in Darlington to be available for sale in places as far apart as London and Edinburgh the following morning.

They chose J. Hyslop-Bell, who was already associated with weekly newspapers in Hartlepool, Stockton and Sunderland, to launch the experiment. Mr Hyslop-Bell determined to produce a daily paper to reach all classes of people and at a price everyone could afford. So it was that, on Saturday 1 January 1870 the *Northern Echo* was founded at ½d per copy.

The timing was good for the newspaper was able to take advantage of the cheap press telegrams which were just coming into existence. This meant that newspapers a long way from London were able to print news of events from across the world very quickly.

To make use of this new facility the *Northern Echo* opened an office in London and thus was able right from the start to provide its readers with news many hours earlier that that printed in London newspapers selling in the North East. This is a feature of the *Northern Echo* that is still significant today.

From the outset the *Northern Echo* was popular with its readers, which Mr Hyslop-Bell found very gratifying. Then, within a year, something happened which far exceeded the paper's original good fortune. It got its first editor; and what an editor!

William Thomas Stead was a clerk at Newcastle when he submitted an article to the *Northern Echo*. In it he compared the administrative institutions of Britain with those of the USA. He was twenty-one years old and comparatively ignorant of newspaper journalism. But he was bursting with nervous energy, good ideas and a ready pen.

In his letter of employment, Stead confirms that the newspaper proprietors told him he could write anything provided it was 'Liberal, non-conformist and Free Trade'.

Stead saw this as a glorious opportunity for 'attacking the devil', and under his editorship the *Northern Echo* flourished, rising from local to national level.

During his nine years at the *Echo*, the intensity of Stead's articles and his penetrating insight into public affairs raised an interest in the paper that reached far beyond the North East. In conversation with Stead, Prime Minister W.E. Gladstone was moved to tell him that: 'To read the *Echo* is to dispense with the necessity of reading other papers. It is admirably got up in every way'.

W.T. Stead went on to edit *Pall Mall Gazette*. He co-founded *Review of Reviews* in 1889 and published a series of children's books and a spiritualist paper. He lost his life on the *Titanic* when it hit an iceberg and sank on 14 April 1912.

Stead was a reforming journalist, a champion of women and a crusader for world peace. His example continues to shine brightly and his chair still stands in the office of the present editor.

In 1895 Edward Daniel Walker, a Darlington businessman, became the proprietor of the *Northern Echo*. He developed the paper's capacity by installing extra printing machinery and the *Echo* became one of the earliest provincial newspapers to change from the traditional method of hand-setting type to the much speedier setting of type by the linotype keyboard casting machine. This method has been updated again, the *Echo* being among the first newspapers to use computer typesetting.

Throughout its early years the *Northern Echo*'s home was a modest terrace in Priestgate. It was there that Stead wrote his popular articles. E.D. Walker's modernising production methods all evolved there.

In 1903, E.D. Walker sold the *Echo* to the newly formed North of England Newspaper Co. Ltd, which was backed by the Joseph Rowntree Trust.

The Chairman of the North of England Newspaper Co. Ltd was Arnold Rowntree and Charles W. Starmer was the manager. Under their control the *Northern Echo* became the foremost newspaper in the region.

As the *Northern Echo* developed, so did Darlington. It became the only place in England to publish and distribute a daily paper with a circulation far in excess of its population. This enabled it to become known as a newspaper town, a proud distinction it still holds today.

In September 1914, the *Echo*'s sister paper the *Northern Despatch* was launched and in 1915 both papers moved to their prestigious new home at the corner of Crown Street and Priestgate. From there both newspapers covered the First World War and other news, giving it a local slant whenever possible. If it was newsworthy, the newspapers belonging to the North of England Newspaper Co. Ltd covered it; and always the same standard of care and accuracy was given to local events as to world news.

In 1915 the *Northern Echo* gave full coverage to a piece of news of particular interest to Darlington, Edmund Backhouse, a Quaker, became Darlington's first MP.

The First World War affected people in different ways. While some Darlingtonians tried to forget its horrors by adopting a hedonistic lifestyle, others were reduced to selling matches on street corners. All these aspects of life in the 1920s and '30s were recorded faithfully and objectively by the *Northern Echo*.

The *Northern Echo* champions the causes of its readers, especially those unable to stand up to strong forces in society for themselves. It is renowned for its determination to promote the region it serves so well. It is an independent paper, completely separated from all political parties, pressure groups and vested interests. It is a paper the reader can trust.

In 1918 Charles Starmer and his business associates founded the Starmer Group and the *Northern Echo* and its associated newspapers became an important part of this organisation.

In 1927 the Starmer Group, merged with Lord Cowdray's influential London newspaper *The Westminster Gazette* to form the Westminster Press.

In 1933 Sir Charles Starmer died and while the Westminster Press moved to Fleet Street, but the newspaper production was still based at Darlington.

Sir Charles Starmer was an outstanding man. Born in Cleveland, he joined the staff of the *Echo* in its Hartlepool office where he dealt with advertising, circulation and several other jobs. He dealt with all those responsibilities with the same enthusiasm he displayed as the first manager of North of England Newspaper Company and later, as managing Director of the Westminster Press.

He was devoted to public service, was twice Mayor of Darlington and Liberal MP for Cleveland. In 1917 he was knighted. He settled in Darlington, which became the scene of his business success.

In 1929, the *Northern Echo*, wishing to improve the lot of local children, many of whom were underprivileged, introduced the Children's Ring, a fun club which gave an added sense of belonging to a caring society. On Saturday 21 November 1929, a Nignog membership coupon appeared in the *Northern Echo*. Anyone forwarding a signed copy to Uncle Mac care of the *Northern Echo*, would become a member and receive a metal Nignog badge. Uncle Mac was snowed under with signed coupons and letters of encouragement. Once again the *Northern Echo* had hit the popularity jackpot.

Luther Worstenholm and Albert Clayton were both long serving editors of the *Northern Echo*, the former serving for eighteen eventful years, the latter for nineteen years.

In 1937 the *Echo*'s sister paper the *Evening Despatch*, had a major scoop. On 11 December 1936, Edward VIII abdicated, the first English King to do so since Richard II in 1399. He did so because he felt he could not carry on without the woman he loved, a twice-divorced American called Mrs Simpson, who could never be queen. Following his abdication and now Duke of Windsor, Edward went to France, where he married Mrs Simpson. The person who conducted the service was a Darlington vicar, who gave the exclusive story, along with world exclusive pictures, to the *Evening Despatch*.

In 1961 Harold M. Evans became editor of the *Northern Echo*, a position he held until 1965 when he left Darlington to become editor of the *Sunday Times*. Under his editorship, the *Northern Echo* became one of Britain's most successful campaigning newspapers. In the mid-1960s a local businessman, Herbert Woolf, launched a campaign to clear the name of Timothy Evans, who had been wrongly hanged for murders committed by John Christie at No. 10 Rillington Place in London. Harold Evans took up the campaign and it led to the abolition of the death penalty.

During 1987–8 the *Northern Echo* won thirteen major journalistic prizes. These included Regional Newspaper of the Year, Reporter of the Year and several Design awards.

In 1989, the ageing presses at Darlington were closed down and the *Echo* was printed on new colour presses at York. New equipment was installed at Darlington and this made North of England Newspapers one of the most modern newspaper publishers in the world. Its nerve centre remained in its Priestgate offices, Darlington.

Today's editor of the *Northern Echo*, Peter Barron, continues the vital work of ensuring that the paper maintains its essential role of keeping its readership fully informed regarding local, regional and national matters and that its popularity is maintained. To this end Mr Barron has recently introduced two innovations. The first concerns content. There are some 1,500 Poles living in and around Darlington. To make them feel welcome and at home, the *Echo* now carries a column in Polish every Thursday for their benefit, and it has been very well received. The second has changed the *Echo* from broadsheet to tabloid, which most readers prefer.

The *Northern Echo* continues to fulfil its role as a regional morning paper for the North East and is proud of its independence and never being afraid to speak its mind. It is devoted to the interests and the wellbeing of the region it serves so well, its people and the newspaper town that is its home.

DARLINGTON'S TWENTIETH-CENTURY JEWELS

Not all Darlington's leisure activities are *al fresco*. The town offers many ways of taking one's ease that are not affected by weather conditions.

Swimming is a good example. Darlington's first public baths were built to provide hot water, a degree of privacy and recreational facilities at a time when few houses had bathrooms. They were sited in Kendrew Street and the swimming baths were open to the sky until 1889 when a roof was added. Mixed bathing was not permitted until 1932. In 1933 Gladstone Street Baths were built and they were the most up to date baths in the North East at the time. The swimming baths were floored over during the winter months and used as a concert area or as a dance floor. When the Dolphin Centre was built, Gladstone Street Baths were declared redundant and, in January 1983, demolished.

From the 1920s the cinema business throughout Britain really took off, reaching its peak in about 1950. At that time Darlington had many cinemas. J. Arthur Rank controlled the two largest cinema circuits in Britain, Odeon and Gaumont, Odeon being the larger of the two. As television gradually captured cinema audiences and cinemas began to close, if a town like Darlington had both Odeon and Gaumont cinemas, it was the Gaumont that had to close because it belonged to the smaller circuit. Now Darlington has only one cinema, the Odeon in Northgate.

Quakers have never been theatre enthusiasts. To their way of thinking a theatre is a den of iniquity and thespians are beyond the pale. So it is surprising that Darlington has been associated with three of them.

Until the early nineteenth century performers coming to Darlington did their acting in a large tent. Then a wooden structure was set aside for them in the Clay Row area of the town. In about 1840 a long room in Tweddell's Yard was made available for them. This was fine until the gallery collapsed during a performance, injuring some of the patrons. The Quakers put it down to God's displeasure. In 1858, much to the annoyance of the Quakers, another theatre was built which presented a different play every night. It was called the Barn Theatre and it occupied a wooden building behind the Green Tree Inn, Skinnergate. It soon died a death.

In 1865 Darlington's first Theatre Royal was built in Buck's Close. Its seating, wooden benches, was unpopular with the patrons and the theatre quickly failed. A new Theatre Royal, was built in 1881 in Northgate but it soon burned down. In 1887 a third Theatre Royal was built. It survived, presenting plays, music hall and films, until the mid-1930s when it was demolished. In 1936, the Cannon Cinema was built on its site.

The Royal Astoria was built in Northgate in 1873 and became the venue for a variety of events and entertainments as different as music hall, theatre, Salvation Army and cinema. It closed in September 1958 and was demolished.

In 1904 Darlington Corporation was embarking on a road-widening scheme and had demolished many old properties alongside St Hilda's church, making available an excellent corner site adjacent to Borough Road. That April, the Darlington Hippodrome Co. Ltd. purchased this corner site and had Darlington Hippodrome theatre built on it.

At that time Darlington's population was about 50,000 and it already had a 1,000-seater theatre in business, so to open another one was decidedly risky. Yet the project went ahead and on Monday 2 September 1907, in the presence of the Mayor and members of the council, the New Hippodrome and Palace of Varieties was formally opened.

The theatre was managed by Signor Rino Pepi, who also managed the Tivoli, Barrow-in-Furness and, within a year, would also manage the Hippodrome theatres at Middlesbrough and Shildon.

Signor Pepi was an outstanding theatrical personality who was born near Florence, Italy, into a wealthy family and abandoned his studies to become a quick-change artist. He married a half-Irish widowed countess and it was she who taught him English. In 1895 he was at the London Pavilion for three months and toured Britain and Europe to great acclaim. Then aged 41 and at the height of his career, he gave up performing for a career in theatre management. He moved to Darlington in 1907, when his company took a lease from the Darlington Opera House and Empire Ltd, which owned the Hippodrome theatre, which was being built. Signor Pepi was a much loved, generous man who liked the horses and moved to Darlington because the theatre was not too far away from a racecourse. It was the only theatre he controlled when he died in 1927.

The years following Signor Pepi's death saw the rise of the cinema and what in those days was called the wireless. Their impact on the theatre was severe. In Darlington, the Hippodrome fell on hard times and, early in 1933, it closed. In October of that year, the Hippodrome reopened with *No, No, Nanette*, but the optimism was unfounded and the theatre very quickly went dark again.

In 1934, Edward J. Hinge, a Newcastle cinema-owner, leased the Hippodrome as a part-time cinema, showing films and putting on variety on alternate weeks. It was not a success and in 1936 Hinge Productions Ltd took over the lease and introduced more variety. Many big names like George Formby, the Two Leslies and Lew Stone and his Band came to Darlington but the theatre continued its decline. Many of the shows were of a high standard but the response of many audiences was poor.

During the Second World War the theatrical theme changed in Darlington. War-time productions like *Don't Blush, Madam* provided popular entertainment for nearby garrisons. Straight plays like *I Am A Camera* by John Van Druten, were interspersed with well known names like Tommy Cooper, Cardew Robinson and stripper Phyllis Dixey. Yet the bloom had gone. Even *Peek A Boo* could not save the Hippodrome.

For many difficult years Teddy Hinge struggled with the ailing Hippodrome, then, on 16 June 1956, he called it a day and the Hippodrome closed its doors for seemingly the last time.

For almost two years the Hippodrome remained dark, gathering dust, while Darlington's theatre lovers waited for it to be demolished. Yet some were not prepared to accept this sad situation. They were members of Darlington Operatic Society who, now that the theatre was closed, found themselves without a home. It was an impossible situation and they resolved to do what they could to reopen the theatre. For two years they cleaned the building and in April 1958, reopened it with *White Horse Inn*. It was a brave and well worthwhile move because it marked a change for the better.

Following protracted negotiations, Darlington Operatic Society formed a non-profit making company called Darlington Civic Theatre Ltd in August 1958. Its purpose was to rescue and run the Hippodrome which they renamed the Civic Theatre. It was to be run by unpaid, voluntary help.

In the beginning, there were many almost insurmountable setbacks. Yet a committee under Alderman Thompson refused to be daunted by them. Slowly they attracted the interest of the general public with Darlington Operatic Society putting on three presentations a year and all-in wrestling and other promotions filling many of the remaining empty weeks. It was not an inspiring situation but, at least, the theatre was remaining open.

Darlington Civic Theatre Ltd had its lease renewed in 1961 and, on 10 November 1964, Darlington Corporation bought the Civic Theatre for £8,000.

In August 1965, Janet Verrill was appointed secretary and manager of the Civic Theatre, a temporary appointment. The council now decided that the theatre needed a full-time professional manager and, in September 1965, Donald Hamilton-Moore was appointed.

In 1965 the theatre was officially changed to Darlington Civic Theatre. Everything else about it remained as it was. It remained a regular venue for touring companies and its future remained in the balance.

The Civic Theatre's main entrance has above it an ornamental tower 63ft high. An ornamental portico ran along its main façade, blending rather well with the building's red bricks. For sixty years the portico graced the theatre until, one day, an ICI tanker, turning into Borough Road, crashed and destroyed it. This accident enabled the front of the theatre to be remodelled.

Inside, the theatre was a mess. Its floors and seats were loose and major alterations to the auditorium needed to be made before it was fit for use. Repairs cost £20,000 but now, at last, the theatre had a licence. Although open once again and giving regular performances, many were of poor quality, youth theatre groups, Scout Gang Shows and the like. Moreover the Civic Theatre closed during June, July and August every year.

Peter Tod, aged 24, was chosen to succeed Donald Hamilton-Moore and this made him the youngest theatre director in the country. He had absolute dedication, boundless ability and the theatre was his life.

Within five years he had confounded all the sceptics by increasing the number of bums on seats from an approximate annual 20 per cent to an amazing 84 per cent. While the number of seats sold in other local theatres fluctuated, those of Darlington's Civic Theatre remained constantly good. Soon the Civic became the most successful theatre in the North East and it became acclaimed throughout British theatrical circles.

With the Civic Theatre doing so well, Peter Tod managed to get extra grant aid from Darlington Council and Northern Arts and with this he was able to negotiate a prestigious opening of plays with London-based Triumph Theatre Productions, which provided material for superior to anything seen before at the Civic Theatre.

All this was fully recorded in the press, in particular in the *Northern Echo* and the interest created ensured that more people became aware of the important theatrical development taking place in Darlington.

Like many theatres, the Civic has its supporters club, the Friends of the Civic Theatre. It was founded in 1965 with 236 members and now has more than 460 members. Down the years Friends of the Civic Theatre has been a tremendous asset to the Civic and its involvement has been multitudinous and varied. When, for example, washing machines and spin dryers were needed for visiting companies, Friends of the

Civic Theatre found the finance to purchase them. When the Civic's curtains became a mouldy disgrace, it was the Friends that replaced them with new ones.

Many of the Civic's much-appreciated facilities would not have been acquired without the help of Friends of the Civic Theatre. Collectively, its members do a splendid job.

But what sort of theatre is the Civic from a performer's point of view? Ken Dodd, OBE, thought by many to be one of Britain's finest comedians, has entertained at the Civic for a great many years. It is a theatre he loves and when he celebrated its 75th birthday on 2 September 1982, he had this to say about Darlington and its jewel of a theatre:

The first time I approached the town of Darlington from the A1 I was amazed. Never having ventured before, into this part of North East Britain, I thought I would come into a land of whistles, signals, shuntings, hooters and railway engines racing through the streets and that the theatre would be a converted locomotive shed. In fact I discovered that Darlington is a lovely town – a fresh, clean, friendly place (the inhabitants are exactly the same) and the theatre is a beautiful emporium of fun and happiness. You can tell as soon as you walk through the stage door that it is loved.

LEISURE: DARLINGTON FOOTBALL CLUB

The town in which the *Northern Echo* is based is a very pleasant one, centred on its ancient market place. Its roads and streets are wide and many of them are lined with green verges and trees. Darlington has a lot going for it.

Before Darlington developed Feetham's Field, a very large area in idyllic surroundings, spread along the eastern edge of the town. Twice-yearly hirings were held there, sales and auctions took place there regularly and it was in Feetham's Field that the occasional military display was held.

As Darlington developed, Feetham's Field diminished, Victoria Road was built through it and Darlington Cricket Club and Darlington Football Club were established there.

Darlington Cricket Club's first ground was at Park Street until 1866 when it rented land from John Beaumont Pease at Feetham's. Twice W.G. Grace, played there, once in 1875 and again in 1907. When Feetham's came up for sale in 1896, Darlington Cricket Club bought it.

In 1883 Darlington Football Club was formed and, in 1889, it became one of the ten original members of the Northern League. In 1908 the Club turned professional and founded the North Eastern League. In the 1912/13 season Darlington Football Club became champions of the League.

The club became a limited company in 1921. Since then it has struggled with financial problems.

When land at Feetham's came up for sale, the club members managed to raise the purchase price and transferred the ownership to a trust.

On several occasions the club has reached the last sixteen of the FA Cup and it got into the Second Division in the mid-1920s.

But most of its life has been a struggle against financial crises, relegation and even re-election.

One of 'Darlo's' favourite players was Alf Common who had a brilliant career during the early years of the twentieth century. In 1902 he became the youngest player ever to win an FA Cup winner's medal. But Alf became known as much for his predictions as for his skill with the ball. He made a prophecy that Darlington Football Club would never go far while they were playing at Feethams: and so it came to pass.

In 1960 floodlighting was installed at Feethams, which enabled the Quakers to move away from daylight-only matches. The first floodlit match was played on 19 September of that year. On the following day, 20 September, the ground's West Stand was completely destroyed by fire. The club had to wait until 1998 for a new very expensive stand.

On 3 May 2003, Darlington Football Club played its last match at Feethams. The opposition was Leyton Orient and the result was a 2–2 draw. The match was outstanding, a fitting end to 120 years of Feetham's history.

From now on home to Darlington Football Club would be a huge stadium on Neasham Road, just outside town. The requirements had been set out in a legally binding agreement in 2000 and after planning permission had been granted it was accepted that the Neasham Road stadium would not open until all the planning conditions had been met. But this did not happen. The new ground opened in August 2003, without the conditions being completed and with many local planning conditions having been breached.

The council said that taking legal action to block the stadium's opening would have resulted in the loss of the town's football club after 120 years in existence.

The chairman of Darlington Football Club, George Reynolds, was deeply involved in the club's move to the new stadium and his financial contribution was such that the stadium was named the Reynolds Arena.

The club's financial troubles were becoming worse. Following a stormy meeting on 20 May 2005, the Quakers hopes were hanging by a thread. The meeting was adjourned by the administrators until the following Tuesday to allow the validity of claims from major creditors, including chairman George Reynolds, to be investigated. But with the Football League demanding that the Quakers' future be resolved by the following Friday, the club had only two days to find a way out of its seemingly intractable problems.

The club would have been doomed if there had been a final vote on a company arrangement worth a total of £150,000 proposed by the stadium's owner, the Sterling Consortium. But the creditors, including George Reynolds, the Inland Revenue and Hall construction, the Ferryhill Company that had built the stadium, all indicated that they would not back the proposed arrangement.

George Reynolds said, 'I am very disappointed because I want the club to survive.'

Great names of North East football united to put on a show for the beleaguered club: Manager Brian Little, Phil Neal, Tony Mowbray, Steve Vickers, Alan Kennedy, Lee Sharp, Paul Gascoigne, Bryan Robson, Chris Waddle, Kenny Dalglish and Peter Beardsley. Each had represented their club and country at the highest level. All donned the colours of Darlington on 25 January 2004, the day destined to become a key date in Darlington's history, to support the struggle to rescue the club. They faced a celebrity side at Reynolds Arena.

All Darlington became involved and many fundraising events to save the club were organised. The Quakers auctioned their official team bus and girls from Polam Girls' School swapped their uniforms for Quakers' colours in a bid to help the town's football club raise cash.

As embattled Darlington Football Club entered its hundredth day in administration, hopes for its survival was still in the balance.

In 2004, George Reynolds quit his position as chairman of Darlington Football Club, leaving a legacy of debt. The Quakers were in the position where they could be extinct within six weeks.

Sterling Consortium remained in control of Darlington Football Club and, at long last, on 11 September 2004, Darlington Football Club relegated its financial troubles to history.

SOUTH PARK

Darlington has no less than nineteen parks, green spaces and recreational grounds, of which South Park, covering 20 acres, is by far the largest.

In 1636, the year farmer James Bellases of Owton, near Hartlepool, made his will, Poor Howdens was a copyhold farm on the south side of Darlington. Poor Howdens was another of James Bellases farms and when he died in 1640, the farm was administered by the Select Vestry of St Cuthbert's Church, which it continued to do for the next 200 years.

By the middle of the nineteenth century, mainly because of building by the Pease family, the people of Darlington were finding it increasingly difficult to walk in pleasant surroundings. So Joseph Pease prevailed upon the Town Commissioners, of whom he was one, to hire Poor Howdens Farm for £32 per annum. A lease of twenty-one years was granted provided the area would be kept in grass and that a number of gentlemen would stand security for the rent.

Joseph Pease made a large contribution to the initial planting of trees for the new park and donated 100 tons of slag for surfacing the footpaths.

The park was opened in 1853 as Bellases Park and one of its rules was that no games were to be played there on a Sunday.

In 1877 Darlington Corporation purchased the park from the Trustees of the Poor Howdens Charity and it became known as Peoples Park. At that time it lay some distance south of Darlington town.

Much later, it became known as South Park and down the years more land was added until it reached its present size of 93 acres.

In 1880, that part of South Park nearest to the town, the south-west corner, was developed as a sport and show ground. Shrubberies were planted there and it had direct access to the town.

In 1921, a boating lake was created there at a cost of £7,200 and it was in regular use until about 1947 when the last boat was taken out. Some ten years later the lake was filled in and a new course for the River Skerne was created.

The whole south-western half of South Park is arboreal. Trees and shrubs are everywhere. They edge the River Skerne, the park's lake with its wooded island and all the paths. The trees are of great variety and include two giant redwood, native to California. The redwoods in South Park are mere infants and should outlive the lot of us.

Flowing gently through South Park, as if reluctant to leave such pleasant surroundings, the River Skerne, passes among other things, a terracotta fountain, a sensory garden and a Victorian bandstand, which Darlington Corporation purchased from Walter Macfarlane and Co. of Glasgow in 1893 for £279. In September 2004 the bandstand was dismantled and returned to Glasgow where it underwent complete restoration as part of the Lottery Funded Restoration of South Park.

Thanks to the multi-million pound Heritage Lottery Funded Restoration Project, which took place from 2003 to 2006, South Park underwent a transformation which returned it to its original Victorian splendour. The transformation also provided exciting new facilities for the twenty-first century.

Every spring the verge along Grange Road explodes in a riot of colour when the crocus season arrives. It lasts until the flowers die and during that time the lives of all who see this superb display of colour are enriched.

In their different ways both South Park and the crocus walk brighten the town.

The Darlington team that reached the last sixteen of the FA Cup in the 1910/11 season.

On 20 September 1960, the day after floodlighting was installed at Feethams football ground, the west stand was completely destroyed by fire.

Spreading the news, Darlington FC-style.

Spot the ball, neither the players nor the spectators seem to know where it is.

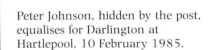

Peter Johnson, hidden by the post, equalises for Darlington at Hartlepool, 10 February 1985.

Playing a nice, clean, game of footer at Feethams.

North Lodge Park, 1932.

A swan and some Canada geese are not too happy about the frozen lake in South Park.

Colin Inness and John Riding caring for the flowers and plants at the Corporation greenhouses in South Park, Darlington, 27 March 1965.

A winter wonderland. Alongside the River Skerne in South Park, 12 November 1976.

Snow heavy on the bough and carpeting both sides of the Skerne in South Park sets off to perfection the waders, 20 February 1981.

This part of South Park, including the Tower Lodge and the flower beds in the foreground, was laid out in 1853 'under the auspices of the local board'. The clock on the tower was installed in about 1900 in memory of William Potts, a local clockmaker.

Canada geese, swans and mallard highlight the bewitching quality of the lake in South Park.

Darlington's imposing Theatre Royal in Northgate just before it was demolished. In 1937 the Cannon cinema was built on its site.

A full house at Darlington Civic. Under the direction of Peter Tod, right, the Civic Theatre enjoyed more full houses it had ever known before.

The exterior of the Hippodrome, which is now Darlington Civic Theatre.

Dame Margot Fonteyn brings a magical evening of ballet to the Civic Theatre, January 1976.

Ken Dodd and William Macdonald celebrate the Civic Theatre's 75th birthday, 1982.

Hilda McCallum with a 1907 original programme from the New Hippodrome, now the Civic Theatre.

Box office girls Margaret Walker, Janet Murray, Pat Fawcett, Elizabeth Carey, Jill Pritchard, Rose Hutchinson and Dorothy Hodgson, Civic Theatre, 11 April 1984.

Director's secretary Betty McFall with other office staff, (left to right) Brenda Fryer, Anne Watson and Pat Fawcett, Civic Theatre, 24 August 1987.

The new upstairs bar at the Civic Theatre, 29 October 1990.

John Murray with knife, presenting a cake on the closure of the Civic for renovations, with the cast of *Cinderella*, 31 January 1990.

Restoration work starting at the Civic Theatre, 9 February 1990.

The Civic Theatre ready for reopening after refurbishment, October 1990.

Darlington Civic Theatre Director, Brian Goddard, (centre) receives two £2,000 cheques for disabled seating sponsorship from Derek Myers (left) MD of Wiltshire Northern and John Parsons, Chief Executive of Darchem Ltd, 20 June 1990.

Jimmy Cricket, Julia Rogers and *Northern Echo* competition winner, Nicola Jane Booth switch on Darlington's Christmas lights on High Row, 23 November 1992.

An evening of pure enchantment from the Moscow City Ballet at the Civic, 5 November 1993.

At the Civic, the stage is swept before the show begins. Then the sweeper makes his exit, actors take over and the magic begins.

The attention of this Civic Theatre audience has been captured by what is happening beyond the proscenium arch. There's not a wandering eye in the house.

Bulmer's stone, Darlington's oldest monument, is a large piece of shap granite deposited by a glacier. For many years it lay on the pavement in Northgate before being placed behind the railings of Darlington College because it was becoming a traffic hazard.

Crowds in Tubwell Row line up to see the unveiling of the South African war memorial in 1902.

Geese resting on High Row en route to market, *c.* 1900. Dresser's original shop is seen behind them.

The north end of High Row today. What a difference a century makes.

High Row, August 1951. The original gentle slope has now got a tarmac surface and is partly stepped.

A night shot of High Row, 2 November 1993. Dressers have moved to a larger store occupying a superb central position.

An aerial view of the Cornmill Centre being built, photographed in July 1991. The atrium is clearly seen left of centre. The *Northern Echo* head office is south of the Cornmill Centre, slightly to its right.

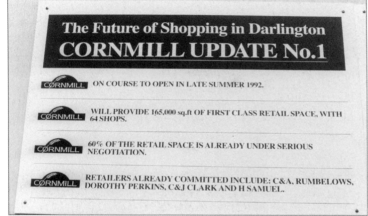

The future of shopping in Darlington? A Cornmill update, 1992.

The Cornmill shopping centre opens in late September 1992.

Darlington on a wet November day in 1967. Making matters worse, a vehicle exiting from Post House Wynd adds to the congestion in Skinnergate.

Post House Wynd, pictured in 1961 before pedestrianisation, is awash with pedestrians.

DARLINGTON'S PEDESTRIAN HEART

Darlington's other jewel is its pedestrian heart, the area bounded by Bondgate and Northgate in the north, St Cuthbert's Way to the east, Victoria Road to the south and Skinnergate to the west. Ever since it was a small market town, Darlington has spread outwards from this centre. In medieval times Bondgate was a village green surrounded by a few cottages, a forge and a bakehouse. In about 1850, part of the green was fenced off to hold market day cattle. By the 1920s Bondgate had become a very wide thoroughfare.

For many years Darlington had a goodly number of coaching inns and pubs, large and small. It also had its fair share of drunks and this worried the town's Abstinence Society to such an extent that they decided to do something about it. On 10 June 1862 they unveiled a drinking fountain in the middle of Bondgate opposite the entrance to Skinnergate. It was to commemorate its first president, John Fothergill MRCS, who had died in January 1858. The fountain was removed to South Park in 1875.

Trams were routed along Bondgate, the tram lines running along the middle of the wide road. They were superseded in 1926 by trolleybuses whose routes were lined with rows of poles that held the wires that carried the current used to power the trolleybuses. Northgate had been a popular shopping centre for many years. Branches of Marks & Spencer, British Home Stores, Boots and other fine stores are sited there.

In 1984 the first steps were taken to revolutionise Darlington as a modern shopping centre. The idea was to build a two-tier shopping mall linking Tubwell Row with Northgate and bridging Priestgate.

In 1988 Sir Robert McAlpine was awarded the contract to build Darlington's Cornmill Centre and work began on it in 1987. Some 876,000 bricks were used which, if placed end to end would stretch from Darlington to Liverpool. The main construction was a reinforced concrete frame and rumour has it a ghostly apparition supervised every aspect of the construction. Building the centre became a technical challenge owing to problems the ground conditions exposed and because it was built around so many existing buildings. When complete, the Cornmill attracted outside retailers to the town rather than local retailers. In 1994, it was sold by Burton Property Trust to the Prudential Assurance Co. Ltd, who have continued to expand it by introducing more new retailers to the town.

In the early twentieth century when cinemas were taking off, Darlington became renowned for its picture houses, many of which were sited in Skinnergate. One of the earliest cinemas was the Arcade, which opened in Skinnergate in 1912. It was famed for its Westerns, especially those starring Tom Mix, and for keeping its entrance fees to a minimum. It was a winning formula and a year after the Arcade opened, a second gallery was added to the building to give it a greater seating capacity. So great was the demand for cinemas at this time that before the Arcade's second gallery was completed, another picture house was opened alongside it – the Court Kinema. This was a more up-market cinema, a sign of things to come.

It was in 1901 that the first moves leading to today's pedestrian heart began. it was the same year that Darlington's town centre was first lit by electricity. It was then that the slope down from High Row, eastwards was rebuilt on two levels with connecting steps. Between the two sets of steps, a tarmac road was built. For the convenience of pedestrians rows of railings separated the different levels.

In 1922 a Sunderland firm bought the business of Arthur Saunders on 5 High Row and, over the years took over other businesses to become Darlington's largest department store. That firm was H. Binns and Co., known today simply as Binns. Both the vast Binns building and nearby Barclay's Bank have added permanence to High Row and they dominate the surroundings.

For many years High Row has been a favoured gathering place for Darlingtonians celebrating special events. The coronation of King George V was celebrated there in 1910 by the town's senior schoolchildren singing patriotic songs. They were conducted by Mr Hogget from the balcony of the town clock some distance away.

The town's pedestrian heart is not in fact wholly pedestrianised. Several of the town's bus routes still run along Crown Street in both directions to the midway point, where they go along Priestgate to turn left into Prebend Row and left again along Tubwell Row over the River Skerne on the Stone Bridge.

The Joseph Pease statue, Darlington's only portrait monument, was unveiled in 1875. Since before then, the whole of the town centre has been in a constant state of change. This is good because without change stagnation sets in. Many of yesteryear's conditions would not be acceptable today. Likewise some aspects of life today do not compare favourably with days gone by. With progress, the secret is to strike a balance, blending the best of history with a modern lifestyle. Darlington has been lucky. Many towns do not have what are proudly called jewels in their crowns. Some towns have one, Darlington has two: its Civic Theatre and its pedestrianised town centre. Long may they remain.

Pedestrianised Skinnergate, September 1995.

Pedestrianised Post House Wynd,
pictured on a gloomy night in 1986
and only one pedestrian in sight.

The statue of Joseph Pease, pictured on New Year's Eve 1983, has been crowned. It is an improvement on the previous Christmas when vandals put a toilet seat around his neck.

Having had a good clean, the statue of Joseph Pease is back, looking along freshly designed High Row, pictured 20 April 2007.